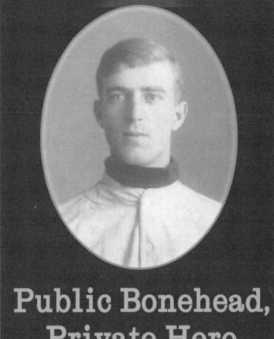

Public Bonehead, Private Hero

The Real Legacy of Baseball's Fred Merkle

Ray —

Merkle Power!

MIKE CAMERON

Best wishes,

MC

Sporting Chance Press™, Inc.
1074 Butler Drive
Crystal Lake, IL 60014
sportingchancepress.com

Photographs appearing in Public Bonehead, Private
Hero were supplied by the National Baseball Hall of
Fame Library, the Library of Congress, the Merkle
family, Ford Motor Company and David Stalker.
Please see the Photographs Credits Table on page 187
for information.

– Contents –

— Acknowledgments —

I am grateful to publisher Larry Norris. He gave me the opportunity to write this book and provided kindness, support and direction along the way.

Special thanks to my brother Tony Cameron and friend Ken Keenan for devoting countless hours to the pre-editing of my work Their help went way beyond skillful refinement of the text. Whenever I meandered, Tony and Ken both understood where this book needed to go and how it should get there. My close friend Ralph Koslik gave me a confidence boost at a vital juncture.

I wanted the reader to get to know the flesh-and-blood Fred Merkle. This would not have been possible without the cooperation of his wonderful family, especially his surviving daughter, Marianne. She opened up to me on highly personal, often painful matters. I am appreciative and touched by her trust and generosity.

I was blessed and inspired by loved ones. Bill Roxworthy, my dear lifelong friend, and Anita Zoerink, my girlfriend and soulmate, both fought—and beat—cancer while I was writing this book. My son Matt, an Army veteran who served our country in Iraq, conquered issues like the courageous, fine young man he is. Amanda, my precious daughter, did more than turn 21; she blossomed into a proud, responsible adult.

— PREFACE —

As a seven year-old in the summer of 1955, my interest in baseball grew from curious to obsessive. Not knowing any better, I rooted for the woebegone Chicago Cubs. My mother took me to a Cubs' game at Wrigley Field. I was awe-struck. This intimate, ivy-adorned "field of dreams" appeared to have been lifted from the country and fitted snugly into a city block. And there was my first hero, Ernie Banks. The New York Giants made mincemeat of the Cubs, but Ernie thrilled me by hitting a homer.

Ernie belted 44 home runs in only his second full season. In a night game September 19 at St. Louis, Banks broke a record by hitting his fifth grand slam off Lindy McDaniel. I was supposed to be asleep but heard it on the radio and gleefully jumped up and down on the bed. That was perfectly okay with my older brother and bunkmate, Tony, who also loved baseball, the Cubs and Ernie. Of course, the rest of the Cubs quickly coughed up a 5–0, sixth-inning lead and lost 6–5.

Being quite young and not very bright, I did not understand that, besides Banks, the Cubs stank. TV announcer Jack Brickhouse was a "homer" who could sell Speedos to Eskimos. Every Cub was either fantastic or promising. We traded away good players for slow, old geezers. Jack convinced me they were still in their primes. The team's youngsters weren't ready and never would be. Jack had me imagining their Hall of Fame induction speeches.

Within a few years, I realized I was being duped. I didn't care. The Cubs' players were generally nice guys. They played hard if not well. I was a baseball fan who lived in the Chicago area and preferred the National League. All the home games were on WGN-TV, and every game was on WIND Radio. I loved the Cubs' uniforms and Wrigley Field. And the Cubs had Ernie Banks.

Banks went on to hit 512 home runs and earn first-ballot enshrinement in Cooperstown. Bill James later said Banks may have been the most valuable player ever during his prime in the late 1950s. He was a sure-handed, everyday shortstop who earned MVP awards in 1958 and 1959 on bad teams by outslugging the likes of Willie Mays and Henry Aaron.

Slowed by arthritic knees in the 1960s, he moved to first base and remained a productive player. New York's Miracle Mets blew past the favored Cubs in 1969, Ernie's last productive season and last legitimate shot to play in a World Series.

"Mr. Cub" was—and still is—arguably the best goodwill ambassador baseball has ever had. He always smiled and spoke of his love for the game. On a terrible weather day before a scheduled single game, Banks famously said "Let's Play Two" to his incredulous teammates in the clubhouse.

Banks was one of the first African-American superstars in the major leagues. He never spoke of the challenges he must have faced. In the 1960s, militants criticized him for not speaking out. He held his tongue.

The man is my kind of hero—not only a great player but a tremendous human being. I have had a picture of Ernie on my bedroom dresser ever since I was a little kid. For me, Banks represents so many good things—joy, class, fortitude, humility and excellence.

As Ernie's baseball career unfolded, I experienced my own joys and trials as a youngster. I wasn't born with many special talents. I was a somewhat smallish, slow-running, white suburban kid. One thing I could do well was to throw a baseball fairly hard and quite accurately with my left arm. I could make the ball move, and I usually could out-think the hitter. I threw all the time. I played sandlot ball with my friends all day. I threw a tennis ball against our barn over and over again. I was a good Little League pitcher.

I did fairly well in high school, but I couldn't throw hard enough to attract scouts. Then something happened the summer after my senior year. I grew to 6-2 and gained physical strength. In American Legion ball, I was suddenly unhittable. I gave up two earned runs the entire season. I struck out 14 batters per seven-inning game. I had lost no movement on my pitches but was probably throwing 84-mph fastballs, with a good chance to add more velocity in the next few years. I had never thought of myself as a big-league prospect. Now I allowed myself to dream.

Then, *poof*, it was over just like that. In fall practice at college, we pitchers were told to throw hard. I was conflicted. I hadn't thrown in two months, but I wanted to make an impression. I threw gas. I almost could feel the fibers in my arm tearing. I was never the same pitcher again. I always had thrown effortlessly. Now, my shoulder hurt. Then my elbow hurt. I kept pitching, usually in pain, for 10 more years simply because I loved it so much.

I have no regrets. I always will have that one summer to remember when I really was a prospect. Most young baseball players never get to experience that feeling.

More than half a century removed from my childhood, I "acquired" a second baseball hero, Fred Merkle.

As a young boy, I remember reading a few of those dry baseball history books. Abner Doubleday invented baseball. Yeah, right. The National League was born in 1876. The American League came along in 1901. The deadball era commenced in the first two decades of the 20th century. Yadda, yadda. For all I knew, Ty Cobb was a choirboy, and Babe Ruth ate salads, drank mineral water and practiced monogamy.

The typical baseball reference book furnished the basic highlights of each year. I remember reading about 1908. My Cubs were actually in a furious three-team pennant battle and played a huge game against the Giants on September 23. This player with kind of a funny name—Fred Merkle—did something on the bases. Not exactly sure what he did. Everyone called him "Bonehead" after that. The Cubs went on to win the National League pennant and the World Series, their last one. Interesting. Then I turned the page and read about the 1909 season. Frankly, I was a whole lot more into contemporary baseball anyway.

A few years ago, I went to my local library and found a good book about the 1908 season and the travails of young Merkle. My obsession with baseball had never abated, and I had become curious about the history of the game. What in the heck had I stumbled upon here? Deadball baseball was fantastic. The players were dedicated, hard-scrabble, irresistible characters. The 1908 pennant races were incredibly dramatic. And what really happened to Fred Merkle?

Well, that triggered my obsessive side. I read everything I could find about 1908 baseball and Fred Merkle. I talked with authors. The good people at baseball's Hall of Fame sent me copies of their files. I contacted Merkle fans. I got in touch with surviving family members, who could not have been nicer. I harbored dreams of writing a movie screenplay.

Something wonderful happened along the way. I found that second baseball hero. I added a picture of Merkle on my dresser right alongside the one of Banks.

Like everyone, I experience challenges, problems and setbacks in my life. When I see Ernie Banks, I feel joy. I look at the picture of Fred Merkle and see strength. His example helps me to believe that I, too, can surmount any of life's inevitable adversities.

I call it "Merkle Power."

I hope this book gives you Merkle Power in your life.

EARLY MERKLE BASEBALL CARD

AMERICA 1908: PIVOTAL, SPECTACULAR, PARADOXICAL

WILBUR WRIGHT IN FLIGHT FROM GOVERNOR'S ISLAND

Americans pretty much went batty throughout 1908, but especially during the first two and a half weeks of autumn.

Wilbur Wright established aerial flight on September 21. National magazine ads introduced Henry Ford's Model T automobile on October 1 and signaled the coming of a whole new world on the ground as well.

Theodore Roosevelt prepared to leave office after seven years as our beloved, take-charge president, leaving voters anxious only a month before they would elect a new leader. Our relations with Japan were strained, but that's exactly where Roosevelt's Great White Fleet—his awesome display of naval might--was headed as it neared the end of its historic around-the-world voyage.

To escape from so many weighty realities, our people stepped up their recent love affair with baseball in that early fall. Passion turned into mania when two tremendous pennant races went right down to the wire.

Curiously, the person everyone talked about the most was not Wright, Ford or even Roosevelt but Fred Merkle, a 19-year-old rookie reserve ballplayer on the New York Giants.

The youngster was perceived to have made a base running mistake in a hugely important game on September 23, which led to another equally historic contest on October 8.

His life would never be the same. Within this backdrop of national and baseball hysteria, Merkle was branded as a "bonehead" and baseball's all-time goat.

Merkle's saga neither starts nor ends on September 23, 1908. We begin by gaining a greater understanding of what the country, baseball and the man himself were like leading up to that fateful day.

IMMIGRANTS AWAIT EXAMINATION AT ELLIS ISLAND

STATE OF THE UNION

Immigrants still saw America as the "land of opportunity." They came ashore in record numbers in 1907, further swelling our population. The newcomers found acceptance and assimilation even more difficult than their predecessors. This wave was less educated, spoke different languages and had different religious traditions and darker skin than most Americans.

Many of them arrived at Ellis Island and settled in New York City and its crowded, filthy tenements on the East Side. Millions of immigrants provided cheap labor for the industrial titans of the Gilded Age. They were by no means the only pawns in our society.

Women began to march for their rights but were still 12 years away from securing the right to vote. They were expected to be subservient to their men. A few prominent blacks were at least being heard, but 89 of their brothers were lynched in 1908. The shame of child labor found millions under the age of 16 working long hours and denied an education. The economic playing field was tilted in favor of rich, established white men who sought greater wealth at the expense of everyone else.

The 1890's had not been America's—or baseball's—proudest decade. Journalists known as muckrakers sought reforms by writing articles and books exposing society's ills. They had plenty to write about. The need for change brought on the Progressive Era in the first two decades of the new century. Awareness was raised in the first; reforms took place in the second.

TRANSITIONAL YEAR

New Year 1908 began with both celebration and innovation, ushered in by the first-ever drop of a giant ball from atop the New York Times Building. Our uglier side emerged toward the end of the year. On Christmas day, Jack Johnson easily beat Tommy Burns to become our first African-American heavyweight boxing champion—the very last present most folks wanted from Santa. The mainstream immediately began campaigning for a "great white hope" who could defeat Johnson.

EARLY MODEL T

In the fulcrum year of the Progressive Era, change came at Americans from all directions. The ultimate bully-pulpit force, Roosevelt had made every important decision for his countrymen for seven years. Things would be different, and not necessarily better, without him.

It was a transitional, pivotal and fantastic year but one which evoked all sorts of inner conflict, hence the historians' other description of the era—"The Age of Uncertainty."

The United States was passing Great Britain and Germany as the world's pre-eminent power, but the majority of Americans opposed imperialism. Trust-busting efforts broke up the monopolies, but 2 percent of our people commanded 60 percent of the country's wealth. The muckrakers' efforts notwithstanding, rights for women, blacks and children barely improved. The notion of a "melting pot" nation gained favor, but poor treatment of immigrants continued.

The Wright brothers' planes conjured dreams of flight everywhere from Grandma's house to other planets, but also prescient predictions of military aerial might and potentially deadly world wars. Similarly, Ford's practical, affordable Model T inspired images of an "America on wheels," but caused considerable anxiety in people who were transported primarily by horses, not horsepower.

The nation's middle class enjoyed an improved standard of living and a lifestyle enhanced by one astounding American invention after another. Finally, Americans started to think harder about social issues that went to the root of how we were treating our fellow man and, especially, those less fortunate.

As it usually does, American baseball mirrored American society in 1908. Both were exciting, dramatic, unpredictable, wacky and flawed. Like America itself, baseball was run by powerful men who openly discriminated against blacks, denied workers' rights and fought union representation

America and baseball came of age by the end of 1908 because the sheer excellence of both transcended their many youthful shortcomings. Each stubbornly insisted on enjoying one last year of glorious, rebellious, semi-innocent adolescence. Maturity and enlightenment be damned. Unharnessed brilliance was far more interesting.

"1908 is not the end of an era or the beginning of one. It is, however, the end of the beginning," wrote Cait Murphy, author of the wonderful, whimsical *Crazy '08.*

DIVERSITY, DISPARITY

The population of "America" exploded from 7 million in 1808 to 76.1 million in 1900 to 88.7 million in 1908. We weren't the only America, of course, but we called ourselves that because bigger sounded better. Similarly in baseball, we did not play an international tournament to determine a true "World Series" champion.

Shortcomings in our society did not stem the tide of immigration. The annual rate of 450,000 over the last two decades of the 1800s nearly doubled to 880,000 in 1900-09, peaking at a single-year record of 1.29 million in 1907.

New York City's population swelled to about 4.3 million in 1908, more than double Chicago's estimated 2 million. The greatness of America's two largest metropolises was undeniable, but that didn't stop one side from putting down the other. To many New Yorkers, Chicago was a smelly stockyard outpost in the middle of nowhere. To more than a few Chicagoans, New York was dirty and overcrowded, its residents arrogant and oblivious to the rest of the world. Although the civic squabbles were generally light-hearted, they added another dimension to the bitter rivalry between the National League's New York Giants and Chicago Cubs.

The old reputation of America's cities as purveyors of sin faded as people enjoyed the increased emphasis on theater and the arts. The population was evenly split between urban and rural dwellers. Farmers thrived in a lengthy boom period of high agricultural prices and were proactive in seeking the same modern products and services that were available to their city counterparts.

California was only the 21st most populous state at about 1.5 million. Movies started coming out of Los Angeles in 1908. A few areas in the West were still open to homesteaders. Oklahoma was admitted as the 46th state the previous year, but it cost five tribal nations their independence.

Increasing numbers of blacks fled the South and its vote-quashing Jim Crow laws for jobs in the North. In Kentucky and Tennessee, there were still vigilante "Night Riders" demanding fair prices for tobacco farmers. During a year in which the FBI was founded, outlaws Butch Cassidy and the Sundance Kid allegedly were killed in Bolivia.

The average factory worker made 25 cents (the general admission price for most big-league games) an hour and about $500 per year. The average major-league ballplayer earned $2,500, to an accountant's $2,000. The average cost of a home was $4,500.

The average life expectancy in the U. S. was 49 years. That number was affected by the high number of fatalities suffered in factories and coalmines; epidemic deaths from diseases such as malaria and smallpox; and primitive health care. Doctors made home visits but were not yet highly skilled or paid. More than 95 percent of births took place at home.

The national suicide rate reached an all-time high of 12.6 persons per 100,000. The rate was markedly worse in baseball during the era; 24 people connected with the major leagues—15 of them players or ex-players—took their lives between 1900 and 1920.

The feminine ideal was a fictional creation known as "The Gibson Girl," who had upswept hair, a swan neck, an hourglass figure and a teasingly coquettish demeanor. Among the beauties who posed as Gibson was chorus girl Evelyn Nesbit, the public's main interest in the first "Crime of the Century." Readers couldn't get enough of the newspapers' lurid accounts of two trials over two years. As a witness, Nesbit defended her mentally unbalanced husband, who was accused of murdering her ex-lover. He was found not guilty by reason of insanity and sent to an asylum

The construction of vital bridges enhanced New York City's transportation infrastructure, complementing its four-year-old subway system. A smattering of automobile taxis appeared amid the more common horse-drawn carriages. Surprisingly, 20 percent of women worked outside the home. The divorce rate was 10 percent.

Husbands and wives slept in separate bedrooms. No matter how hot it was, men wore bowler hats and suits with stiff, high collars. Women were covered by long dresses over layers of undergarments and a tight corset. The ladies wore huge, flowered "Merry Widow" hats that exasperated spectators stuck behind him. Both genders were shorter, smaller and noticeably paler, owing in part to dedicated avoidance of sun exposure.

Americans drank Coca-Cola, Pepsi and Budweiser; shaved with Gillette disposable razor blades; sped up household chores with brand-new vacuum cleaners and electric washing machines; and greeted the milkman and iceman.

Scott Joplin, an African-American and improvisational pianist, introduced lively ragtime music, a forerunner to jazz. The first recording of "Take Me Out to the Ballgame" came out in October. Jack Norworth's lyrical ode to Katie Casey, a baseball-crazy fictional lass, eventually became our third most played song, behind "Star Spangled Banner" and "Happy Birthday."

Nickelodeons, so named because admittance cost a nickel, spread throughout all parts of the country. These small neighborhood theaters showed 20-minute silent movies accompanied by live piano or organ music. Vaudeville acts on Broadway ran the entertainment gamut; the only requirement was that they attracted an audience. The Ziegfeld Follies made their controversial Broadway debut the previous year.

Baseball surpassed boxing and horse racing as our favorite spectator sport. Because pro hockey, football and basketball didn't exist until years later, baseball enjoyed a captive audience throughout the year. Fans, anxious for the start of a new season, clustered around the proverbial "hot stove" in the winter to discuss their favorite teams and the latest trades.

Human Locomotive

Roosevelt supported baseball, but he didn't play or like the sport, referring to it as a game for "molly-coddlers." No other politician would dare say that, but it made perfect sense coming from a man so candid, tough and hyperactive.

"At home and abroad, Theodore Roosevelt was the locomotive president, the man who drew his flourishing nation into the future," wrote *TIME* Magazine in its 2006 commemorative edition. No one personified his era like Roosevelt, achieved more in one lifetime, was more full of himself or handled adversity with more courage.

Roosevelt, born with a bad heart, was home-schooled because he suffered from life-threatening asthma. Despite his infirmities, his father commanded him to become physically strong through vigorous exercise. At Harvard, he was an accomplished rower and reached the finals of the boxing championship. Early on, he became an avid and learned outdoorsman, explorer, hunter and naturalist.

On February 14, 1884, Roosevelt, 25, lost his mother and first wife to different illnesses. He refused to talk about it the rest of his life. Two years later, he married his childhood sweetheart. They settled into the estate he built in Oyster Bay, New York. Roosevelt alternately spent his time as a cowboy on his two ranches in North Dakota. More heartache came later when he lost a son—reputed to be his favorite—to World War I aerial combat.

Roosevelt was appointed Assistant Secretary of the Navy in 1897. He resigned the next year upon the declaration of the Spanish-American War to form a volunteer cavalry regiment, dubbed the "Rough Riders." He rose from Lieutenant Colonel to Colonel—which he preferred being called to "Teddy"—and led the famous charges in Cuba up Kettle Hill and San Juan Hill. He ascended Kettle on foot after his horse tired. His macho side emboldened by the triumph, Roosevelt later told his four sons he'd rather see them die than become "sissies."

He was elected New York's governor in 1898 and vigorously fought machine politics and corruption. Two years later, he rose to vice president under William McKinley. In September 1901, Roosevelt, 42, became our youngest-ever president after an anarchist assassinated McKinley.

As president, he invoked the Sherman Antitrust Act against Northern Securities, began construction of the Panama Canal, won the Nobel Prize for negotiating a treaty that ended the Russo-Japanese War, expanded the terms of the Monroe Doctrine that forbade foreign invasion of the Western Hemisphere, dissolved the beef trust, supported the indictment of Standard Oil on antitrust charges, tightened immigration standards, established the first national wildlife refuge and protected for the public 125 million acres of forest land.

ROOSEVELT—NO "MOLLY CODDLER"

Roosevelt, who frequently skinny-dipped in the Potomac during winters, continued to box while he was president until he took a hit that blinded him in his left eye. He told no one and switched to jujitsu. That was nothing. While campaigning in Milwaukee in 1912, Roosevelt was shot in the chest—the bullet penetrating three inches, the blood seeping down his shirt. He finished his entire speech and left the bullet in place the rest of his life.

On an African safari a few months after he left office, Roosevelt and his companions killed or trapped over 11,000 animals and then shipped them back to our museums and zoological institutions. In 1914, he contracted malaria during an expedition through the jungles of Brazil. He was never well again but lived five more years. Roosevelt is the only person to be awarded the Medal of Honor and the Nobel Peace Prize.

PLANES, STRAINS AND AUTOMOBILES

Two days before the "Merkle game," Wilbur Wright permanently reclaimed aerial supremacy for him and brother Orville. Four days earlier, Orville suffered a tragic flight that threatened their life work and reputations. The probable cause of the crash was a broken propeller blade. Orville broke a leg and several ribs. His passenger, Lieutenant Thomas Selfridge of the Signal Corps, died from a fractured skull.

Wilbur quickly set the skeptics straight, flying in Le Mans, France over his long-time competitors and a crowd of 10,000 spectators. He beat his own record of 39 minutes, eclipsed Orville's record of 75 minutes and finally landed in semi-darkness 91 minutes and 61 miles later to salutes of universal acclaim

On the 366th and last day of the leap year, Wilbur made a two-and-a-half hour flight, further securing the Wright brothers' place alongside Thomas Edison and Alexander Graham Bell on the top rung of world-changing inventors.

On October 1—smack-dab between the Merkle game and a riotous, pennant-deciding tiebreaker—Henry Ford's advertisement for his Model T first appeared in magazines, and America's love-hate attitude toward the automobile changed forever. The big eye-opener was the modest $850 cost. The average price of automobiles was $3,000—three times the annual salary of the typical middle-class worker.

Only about 200,000 automobiles chugged around in 1908. Most were unreliable, driven in cities and owned by affluent men who could afford them as show-off toys. Modest speed limits didn't provide much of a deterrent because of lax enforcement. Curiously, the newspapers criticized the vehicles as an "urban menace," not so much their reckless drivers. An ad for Dewar's scotch glorified drinking while driving

Ford, a conservative man, simply sold mobility to every family. The Model T was black and unattractive but functional. Like the Wrights, Ford took the internal-combustion engine—another breakthrough American invention—and built a machine in and around it better than the competition. Orders exceeded 10,000 for the balance of 1908. By 1927, the Model T's last production year, total sales surpassed 15 million.

Jack Johnson was easily the most controversial man of the era. Black, outspoken, brash and determined to do whatever he wanted, he represented a new—and threatening—kind of sports superstar. If the defiant Muhammad Ali of the 1960s was a decade ahead of his time, his idol—Johnson—was at least six ahead of his.

Johnson held the crown for seven years, beating a succession of "great white hopes." His style of patiently, methodically wearing down opponents and then putting them away in the later rounds was widely viewed as devious and sadistic. He routinely slept with white women, married three and openly bragged about all of them in an era when it was dangerous for a black man to even look at a white gal. Johnson had a quick wit and a heavy foot on the gas pedal. A police officer stopped him for speeding and fined him $50. Johnson tossed the cop a $100 bill and told him he would be returning at the same speed.

The mainstream preferred to follow different adventures. Robert Peary embarked from New York by ship in his third effort to reach the North Pole. By next spring, he sent word that he had succeeded; he probably did. His challenger, Frederick Cook, made the same claim; he probably didn't. The evidence isn't compelling either way.

The so-called Great Race featured automobiles attempting to traverse an ill-planned 20,000-mile course from New York to Paris via tundra and quagmires. Of 15 scheduled drivers, 6 showed up and 3 finished. Alaska proved impossible—surprise—necessitating a route change. The vehicles broke down regularly in what became more of a human-endurance test. Finishing in 169 days with his Thomas Flyer, George Schuster made it a victory for America.

The whole year must have felt like a race. Jim Rasenberger, who wrote the rollicking *America 1908* described it as a "hell of a ride around the sun" and a "spectacular, pivotal year in American history."

Rasenberger added, "It's safe to assume that many Americans entered 1908 having never seen a movie, ridden in an automobile or grasped that humans could fly—and ended the year having done all three."

Not incidentally, 1908 also was the year in which "Merkle" became a verb.

HARRY WRIGHT—BASEBALL PIONEER

KNICKERS TO BONKERS

FOOD VENDORS OUTSIDE EBBETS FIELD

A t any given time during a game in 1908, a baseball more resembled a cow pie.

Baseballs, which lacked springy cores, gradually turned darker, mushier and misshapen from repeated bashings. They often stayed in play past any reasonable notion of shelf life because umpires were allotted only three new balls before each game.

The ball itself was a hot topic in the preseason. The sport's honchos told pitchers that their legal spitballs were absolutely disgusting. They implored players to spray tobacco juice in another direction to keep the balls whiter longer. Nothing changed.

A year before the new steel-and-concrete era of construction, ballparks were still the same rickety wooden firetraps of the late 1800s with some extra seating.

Security was scant despite burgeoning attendance and the continued practice of seating fans who drank and gambled openly on the field. They joined the players in abusing the umpire.

Players were conditioned to watch out for bottles thrown at their heads. Outfielders scrummed with fans for rolling extra base hits.

If a team had a full-time trainer, he knew little about medical treatment beyond basic rubdowns and bandaging knees, and his duties included attending to uniforms and equipment. In an emergency, there was probably a "doctor in the house," but he likely obtained his license from a quickie medical school with astonishingly low standards.

Newspapers—as many as 6 to 10 in the major cities—fiercely competed for readers. Feeling the heat from their publishers, editors sought colorful baseball stories. Many didn't know the difference between a strike and a ball, but they were well aware of the sport's growing popularity. The result was a permissive brand of journalism.

Sportswriters embellished, omitted and often botched game highlights. They showed obvious bias toward the home team. They hyped their favorite players and ripped those they didn't like. They impugned the visiting team, physically impaired and dark-skinned—all in quite jocular, flowery prose.

Blacks had been excluded from the major leagues for 24 years and would be for another 39.

LOOSE REINS

The sport had no commissioner; a timid, harried National League president on the threshold of madness; and ruling committees composed of team owners with conflicting self-agendas.

This was 1908 baseball—a misguided, undisciplined adolescent with a gap-toothed smile, Huckleberry Finn gone wild.

All of which was fitting because everything else in 1908 was just like that. Promising, exciting, loopy, askew, incomplete.

We'll look back at 2010 in another 102 years and poke fun at ourselves, too.

Baseball had a designated *what?* The leagues played by different rules? They played an exhibition game to determine home-field advantage in the World Series?

Baseball and America are still works in progress, and they always will be. The fans didn't know what 1908 baseball wasn't, and they fell madly in love with what it was, which was pretty darned terrific.

Despite its many warts, baseball deserved the tremendous upswing in popularity it received in 1908. After decades of tumultuous growing pains, it had been stable for the past seven years. Stability bred familiarity.

Historians set the beginning of the modern era at 1901 for good reason. The American League burst onto the scene, quickly proving the equal of the established National League.

In the game's last major rules change, the NL began counting foul balls as strikes one and two in 1901, and the AL followed suit two years later. Forevermore, this was how the greatest game on earth would be played.

The 1908 season would be the eighth with two leagues and 16 teams, the fifth with no franchise shifts and a designed 154-game schedule and the fourth consecutive (fifth in all) culminating in a World Series between the two league pennant winners.

It was all so perfect that essentially nothing would change for 53 years.

Even before the amazing pennant races of 1908 took shape, coverage of the sport was on the rise, attracting more followers. *Baseball Magazine* was born that year.

Tracking baseball up to 1908 is like trying to follow a knuckleball. It fluttered, dipped, rose, baffled…and finally, inevitably arrived.

DIAMOND IN THE ROUGH

Whether for fun or food, human beings have been whacking something with a stick since the beginning of humanity. Of course, cavemen did not have to learn the strike zone or the art of bunting. Later on, Homo sapiens got civilized and traded loincloths for knickers. The British started playing rounders and cricket, neither of which looked liked American cups of tea.

In the early 1800s, Americans favored town ball, which featured a square infield, teams of up to 15 players (but maybe 50 on any given day), loose rules and a languid pace. Someone needed to do a heckuva lot better than that.

Alexander Cartwright, a member of a New York team called the Knickerbockers, envisioned a quicker-tempo game more in tune with America's bustling energy. In 1845, Cartwright devised 20 rules that formed the basis for baseball. Joy was his middle name—and exactly what he brought us.

His rules included three outs to a side, three strikes for an out, nine persons per team, fair-foul boundaries and a diamond bound by four bases 90 feet apart. Incorporating those rules, the Knickerbockers and the New York Nine played the first recognized baseball game at Hoboken, New Jersey, in 1846.

Kind of a stuffy affair, but Cartwright's game was a keeper. Later on, he traveled westward to promote baseball. As the sport turned professional, he railed against gambling as an evil to be quashed.

No baseball historian questions Cartwright's niche as baseball's ground-level pioneer, but several dispute certain specifics. Persuasive evidence indicates: the Knicks already were playing by some of the aforementioned regulations before the first official game, Cartwright's list doesn't mention some of the key rules for which he was credited and the sport gradually implemented quite a few of them over the next dozen years.

In 1857, a committee that oversaw many of New York's baseball teams tweaked one rule and decided that a game would be played nine regulation innings to determine a winner rather than the first team to score 21 runs.

Henry Chadwick, a British-born cricket fan, watched an early game of baseball and became an immediate convert. He introduced the box score in 1863, kept adding statistics (such as batting average and earned run average) to measure players against one another and devised a system for the average fan to keep score of a game.

Chadwick, the acknowledged "Father of Baseball," became the most prominent sportswriter of the century and helped to write and edit baseball's formative rules manuals. In 1862, he eliminated the rule that allowed balls caught on one bounce to be counted as outs.

Everyone from kids to women to farmers started playing baseball after the Civil War. The soldiers played regularly and brought the game home with them.

The pitcher—regarded as just another fielder—threw underhanded and placed the ball high or low, depending on the hitters' wishes. In 1867, Candy Cummings started throwing a curveball, and pitchers began to cheat toward sidearm and exert more wrist snap.

Catchers wore no gloves or protective equipment. Although they set up 35 to 40 feet behind the plate, they frequently suffered broken noses and cracked teeth.

GOING PRO

Amateur leagues sprang up everywhere in the 1860s. It was hardly a secret that a handful of star players on many teams were paid under the table. Harry Wright, a former Knickerbocker, envisioned a professional game and huge profits to go with it.

In 1869, Wright introduced the Cincinnati Red Stockings, baseball's first all-professional team. Because there was no league, they were a traveling barnstorming squad.

Cincinnati went undefeated for more than a year behind Wright, a brilliant and dedicated baseball man who later led powerhouses in Louisville and Boston.

Thanks to Wright, extra innings were created in 1870. The Red Stockings lost 8–7 to the Atlantics, the best team in the East. The game was tied 5–5 after nine innings. Wright was willing to put his team's winning streak on the line by agreeing to continue play.

Baseball already was destined to be the only sport in which the defense held the ball. Now it was the only game with no clock or time restraint whatsoever.

The National Association was the first professional league. It was a disorganized mess that somehow lasted from 1871 to 1875. Teams made up their own schedules and frequently didn't show up for games.

As the NA teetered, William Hulbert—a coal magnate and baseball entrepreneur—lured Albert Spalding, Boston's ace pitcher, to join his Chicago White Stockings (later the Cubs) by offering him $4,000 and 25 percent of the gate receipts. Spalding brought over three of his Boston teammates and recruited Cap Anson, Philadelphia's young star.

The NA folded, Hulbert started the National League in 1876 and Spalding never stopped promoting baseball and himself. He won 47 games to lead Chicago to the first NL pennant, started wearing a glove the next year and opened a sporting-goods store.

The fears of corruption in the professional game materialized in 1877. The Louisville Grays suspiciously lost seven straight late-season games and blew a big lead to Boston. The *Courier-Journal* pointed fingers. Star pitcher Jim Devlin admitted taking money from gamblers. Hulbert, who had promised an honest game, banned Devlin and three other Grays for life. It would not be baseball's last gambling scandal.

Spalding retired to Chicago's front office at age 28 and moved up to owner three years later upon the death of Hulbert in 1882. He erected a lavish luxury box for himself in Chicago's stands. It included a telephone and a gong to beckon servants. Spalding secretly employed his mother as the team's official scorer.

He introduced the sport's first official rules guide in 1877 and declared that Spalding baseballs must be used for all games because all other brands were of inferior quality. He bought out several sporting-goods manufacturers but continued to market several of their brand names to present the illusion of competition.

The swath Spalding cut through baseball extended to 1907 when he presided over a commission that spun the patriotic fairy tale that General Abner Doubleday, a Civil War hero, invented baseball in 1839 at Cooperstown, a picturesque small town in upstate New York. Doubleday, indifferent about baseball, was at West Point that year. His obituaries mentioned that he disliked outdoor sports.

Baseball is quite confusing. It often wins when it loses and loses when it wins. Whatever integrity it lost with its shameless fable, baseball gained more with Cooperstown as the ideal keeper of its flame.

Several upstart leagues came and went. The American Association (1881-1891) had some staying power but sold a carnival atmosphere of drinking and gambling.

Spalding demanded and won unconditional surrender from the Players' League in 1890, a one-year threat to the owners' imperious rule. There was no fiercer advocate of the reserve clause, which bound players to their current team for perpetuity, negating their bargaining power.

Even when he was one of them, Spalding despised players. Sometimes he had good reason. Mike "King" Kelly was a Chicago star but a heavy drinker and overtly dirty player. Spalding sold him for a record $10,000 to Boston, which loved Kelly.

Leagues of Their Own

Spalding's remaining star was Anson, the game's greatest player of the 1800s. He was an influential voice that reflected baseball's racist attitudes and practices.

Before an exhibition game in 1883, Anson threatened not to play against Toledo unless Moses Fleetwood Walker, its black catcher, was removed. Toledo held firm, and the game was played.

Anson pulled the same thing the next year and got his way. Newark capitulated and took George Stovey, its black player, off the field.

The major and minor leagues then quietly agreed not to sign black players. When Walker retired after 1884, he became the last African-American to play in an integrated professional league until Jackie Robinson, who broke the big-league barrier 63 years later.

The so-called national pastime excluded women, too. There were several women's college baseball teams in the

1860s. The teams were quickly dissolved after observers made a fuss about injuries to the fairer gender.

In the 1880s, baseball aggressively experimented with its rules. It changed the walk rule six times, gradually lowering the number of balls required for a walk from nine to four. There were brief trials with four-strike strikeouts and flat bats.

By the end of the decade, gloves had gained favor and pitchers threw overhand. In 1893, the distance from the pitcher's rubber to home plate was lengthened from 50 feet to the current 60 feet, 6 inches, temporarily ballooning batting averages. In 1900, home plate expanded from a square to a pentagon, pushing batting averages back down.

The NL had a monopoly from 1892 to 1900 and fared poorly. With only one major league, there could be no postseason championship series. Several were popular in earlier years, predating the modern era.

Baseball behavior degenerated from borderline to flagrantly dirty in the 1890s. The Baltimore Orioles won three pennants to Boston's five, but they were the undisputed leaders in high-spiking, tripping, grabbing opponents' belts and jerseys, shortcutting the bases, fighting and openly abusing umpires. When the Orioles got verbal, drunken sailors ran away.

PUGNACIOUS JOHN "MUGGSY" MCGRAW

Baltimore's most pugnacious player was third baseman John McGraw. The youngest of eight children, Mc-
Graw lost his mother and four siblings to diphtheria. His
father beat him often, and he left home for good at age
12. McGraw stood only 5-foot-6 and weighed barely 125
pounds when he became a hard-edged professional ballplayer at 16 years old.

Genteel folks stayed away from the games, perceiv-
ing the players as uneducated, rowdy, drunken Irish low-
lifes. The stereotype was misleading; there were at least as
many decent, upstanding, Irish and non-Irish players who
disliked McGraw's style of play.

The sport had done a complete 180 from its roots— city gentlemen engaging in a clubby game to back-alley ruffian pros out to maim each other. Most fans probably would have preferred to watch B over A, but there clearly needed to be a C.

BASEBALL RIPENS

Meanwhile, Ban Johnson, a large, arrogant man and former sportswriter, was running the smoothest, cleanest league in the professional ranks. Beginning in 1893, he presided over the Western League, a growing minor league.

Baseball was about to get the second big league it so desperately needed, against the wishes of NL magnates conditioned to their own greed, protectionism and internal power plays.

Johnson added several big-market teams in 1900 and renamed his league the American League. In 1901, he added more big-market franchises and declared the AL a major league. He continued his policies of enforcing cleaner play, respect for umpires and better behavior by the players.

The NL already had been caught napping by leaving big-city markets vacant for Johnson and doing little about its dirty play and hooliganism. It then gave the new league another opening by capping player salaries at a then-low $2,400. Several stars quickly jumped to the better-paying AL, and more than 100 players followed them.

This led to a truce and peace agreement after 1902 in which the two leagues were bound to honor each other's contracts. Now on even footing, the AL quickly proved it was better on the field and at the gate. In 1903, the AL—in only its third season as a big-league entity—trounced the NL in attendance by 32 percent and won the modern era's first World Series.

Baseball was in serious trouble before Johnson's crucial contributions of a second league and image makeover. It soared thereafter. Although he came along after the sport was established as a professional enterprise and had its basic rules already in place, Johnson ranks with pioneers Cartwright, Chadwick, Wright, Hulbert and Spalding for his influence on baseball.

The AL's Boston Pilgrims, later the Red Sox, defeated the NL's Pittsburgh Pirates in that first Series. Boston's rabid contingent of Royal Rooters added boisterous merriment to the tourney's successful debut. They were fanatics, which was shortened to fans. That sounded better than "bugs" or "cranks," the previous monikers. Obviously, marketing of baseball needed a little work.

There was no World Series in 1904 because the ornery McGraw, now manager of the NL's pennant-winning New York Giants, refused to play the AL. Johnson inherited the Orioles as part of the AL in 1901 and 1902; he regularly disciplined McGraw, who now held the fiercest of grudges. Nor did McGraw or Giants' owner John Brush—who also hated Johnson—want to risk losing city bragging rights to the New York Highlanders, a late-season AL contender in '04 and potential Series foe.

After the Giants repeated as NL champs in 1905, Brush and McGraw changed their tune and agreed to play AL winner Philadelphia. New York won four of five games, three on shutouts by Christy Mathewson in a six-day span.

The next year, McGraw audaciously outfitted his team in home-and-road jerseys that read "World's Champions" instead of the team's city or nickname. The Giants were now a daily in-your-face billboard for winning the same Series their manager had killed the previous fall.

DEADBALL SOARS

Regardless, the sport was entering the halcyon years of its deadball era.

"Baseball in the years from 1905 to 1919 was soaked in strategy as it never was before and never has been since," said Bill James in his *Bill James Historical Baseball Abstract.*

Home runs were rare and runs hard to come by. The contemporary fan watches highlights of home run after home run propelled by much larger men hitting a tightly wound ball over more reachable fences. This was not that brand of baseball.

Most games took less than two hours and were tight and pitcher-dominated. Scoring was slightly under seven runs per game. In 1908, batters in both leagues hit only .239—the all-time nadir in the NL and the lowest in the AL until 60 years later. There was significant offensive value in one-base advances via bunts, stolen bases and the hit-and-run. Using thick, heavy bats that had very little taper from the barrel to the knob, hitters choked up and often left a space between their hands for better bat control. Batters swung for contact, low trajectory and direction rather than distance.

Wee Willie Keeler previously gained fame for his ability to "hit 'em where they ain't." Place-hitting remained a highly prized skill. Batters hitting the ball low and hard had a better chance to reach base because the small gloves translated to more errors and reduced range. Smart defensive positioning and mental alertness were paramount.

As the game gained more appeal, so did its players. Baseball's rowdy, all-Irish, lowlife image was changing. The ranks became more diverse in ethnicity, geographic origin and level of education. More than 20 percent of players in 1908 had attended college, including six each on the Cubs and Giants. Public interest intensified in star players such as the handsome, mannerly, college-educated Mathewson.

By 1908, it was cool for just about anyone to attend a baseball game.

In the all-Chicago series of 1906, the "Hitless Wonders" White Sox upset the Cubs, four games to two. The

Sox won the AL pennant despite hitting a paltry .230. The powerhouse Cubs breezed to the NL flag with a 116–36 record, a .763 winning percentage that still stands as the best for a regular season. The underdogs' bats got hot at the right time, producing eight runs in each of the last two contests.

Nevertheless, the Cubs were on their way to the greatest five-year run in baseball history and rebounded in 1907 to defeat the Detroit Tigers and their hell-bent, 20-year-old batting champion, Ty Cobb.

The Cubs and Tigers would meet again in 1908, but not before all hell broke loose.

LARRY DOYLE—MERKLE'S CLOSE FRIEND AND TEAMMATE

"Great to Be Young and a New York Giant"

Fred Merkle—A Combination of
Strength and Speed

Finding a gem like Fred Merkle wasn't easy back then. Even the Giants, baseball's most aggressive organization, had only one scout—Dick Kinsella—and he was just a part-timer.

A barber in Michigan mentioned Merkle to Giants' owner John Brush. Brush was only there because he hoped a particular doctor could cure him of a rare disease—locomotor ataxia—that forced him to walk with the aid of two canes.

Merkle, 18, had turned heads in his second season with Tecumseh of the Southern Michigan League. Late in the summer of 1907, he happily signed for $2,500—an enormous sum for a player from Class D, the lowest minor-league classification. He headed directly to the big leagues and the Big Apple.

It was a lot for the youngster to take in. Merkle, a product of the classic American immigration story, had come a very long way in a very short time.

Fred's grandfather, Johann, was a craftsman who grew up in Switzerland and spoke German. He raised three children with his first wife, who died young. The widower married again and had another son, Ernst, in 1865.

Johann, now 55, emigrated from Switzerland with his two older children in 1866. They settled in Iowa at the Amana Colonies, a sprawling religious settlement established by German-speaking settlers and composed of seven villages. His wife and two-year-old Ernst came over the next year and the youngest daughter a year after that.

After Johann passed away in 1871, the family moved to Fowler, Illinois—a small German settlement and farming community six miles from Quincy. Ernst grew up there and graduated from a teachers' seminary. He left at age 19 to teach at Immanuel Lutheran Church in Watertown, Wisconsin. Three years later, Ernst returned to Fowler to marry Anna Amalia Thielman, the daughter of a German immigrant and blacksmith.

Ernst lived and taught classes in a two-story schoolhouse on the church grounds in Watertown. Amalia settled in with him. She gave birth to Carl Frederick Rudolf Merkle on December 20, 1888.

Amid rumors that Ernst was a little too strict with his students, his teaching contract was not renewed in 1889. When Fred was 15 months old, the family moved from Watertown to Toledo, Ohio. Ernst got another teaching job at a Lutheran school and also sold pianos. The Merkles had three more children.

"I think the right word is 'serious'. Fred grew up in a 'serious' atmosphere, raised by intelligent, devout people with 'serious' integrity," said Sue Baxter, his grandniece and the family historian. "Mind your P's and Q's. Do well in school. Work hard. Respect your elders. Don't draw attention to yourself. Do not strike back when others behave badly toward you. Don't stoop to their level. This is built into our wiring."

Fred spoke two languages, studied philosophy and history extensively and was brilliant in advanced algebra. He played the piano and the violin and developed into an expert chess and tournament bridge player. Grantland Rice, the legendary sportswriter, said that Merkle was one of the most erudite players he ever knew.

He was a "bonehead" only if the Three Stooges were rocket scientists.

YOUNG STUD

Americanizing his name to Frederick Charles Merkle, he graduated from Toledo High School in 1905 at age 16. He starred as a running back in football and as a pitcher in baseball. He found time to partake in athletic programs at the YMCA and set a record in the 16-pound shot put that stood for years. He combined strength and speed in a 6-foot-1, 190-pound frame.

Merkle pitched for a Toledo semipro team in 1905 and tried out the next year with Newark of the Ohio-Pennsylvania League. Newark management released him after only a few games. Fred signed as a third baseman with Tecumseh.

Tecumseh shifted him to first base in 1907, and he hit .271 with a league-high six home runs, leading his team to the championship. He also met Ethel Brownson, his future wife.

Upon signing with the Giants, the 18-year-old Merkle now had $2,500 that would spend like $60,000 today. As he packed for New York, he and his pretty girlfriend made plans for her to visit him. Merkle hopped on a train, set foot in the bustling metropolis of more than four million people and realized he wasn't in Watertown, Toledo or Tecumseh anymore.

He took his first trip on the subway to 155th Street and Eighth Avenue. From the platform, he could look down and see his first-ever major-league park. Tucked below

Coogan's Bluff, the Polo Grounds appeared enormous but also intimate and inviting.

Merkle met living legends such as McGraw and Mathewson and the rest of the Giants. They immediately warmed to him, sensing his smarts and sincerity. He wasn't sure where he would be living or with whom, but the Giants had thought of that. He would share an apartment in Manhattan with "Laughing Larry" Doyle, a fun-loving 21-year-old being groomed to play second base. The two hit it right off. They were destined to be close friends and form the right side of the Giants' infield for seven full seasons.

McGraw's team was out of the race in 1907, which wasn't a bad thing for Merkle. Making his debut September 21, the kid appeared in 15 games and got 47 at-bats, hitting a credible .255 that was well above the league average.

The youngster continued to shine the following spring training and made the 17-man roster. Still considered a rookie and still the youngest player in the majors, the 19-year-old continued his watch-and-learn apprenticeship from the bench and played sparingly.

Very early in his career, Merkle became known for his aggressive, head-first slides. Nearly all players led with their feet. His dives stood out even more because he was such a large man.

Merkle was spiked in early July 1908. The dye from his colored uniform sock seeped into the wound. He had an extreme sensitivity to the dye, causing an infection that nearly took his life. His foot swelled to twice its normal size. He avoided amputation only after the second of two surgeries proved successful. Merkle recovered fully and quickly, missing less than a month. He picked up where he left off, playing infrequently but catching eyes.

READY ROOKIE

In its August 22nd edition, *The Sporting Life* featured Merkle on its front page. Among the compliments was his "good judgment on the bases." The *New York Globe* praised him as a "fellow who uses intelligence in everything he does."

Thus, the Giants weren't concerned when young Merkle had to make only his second start of the season—and first one at first base—on September 23, 1908, even though he had fewer than 40 at-bats in just 35 games. Fred Tenney, the regular first baseman, was out for the first time all season with soreness in his back and legs. Merkle's other start was at second base back on June 26.

It was a crucial, tight game on September 23 against the defending World Series-champion Chicago Cubs and stood at 1-1 in the bottom of the ninth inning. Merkle had performed like a seasoned veteran throughout the tense affair, robbing Joe Tinker of a hit with a difficult line-drive catch and coaxing a walk at the plate. He was about to deliver in the clutch.

The Polo Grounds crowd of 20,000 roared its approval as the rookie lashed a long single to right field, sending the runner from first to third base, 90 feet from sweet victory.

Merkle sped around first and considered legging out a double. With two outs and the potential winning run now on third, he wisely put on the brakes—a smart baseball decision but one with unfortunate, life-altering consequences.

The next batter lined a rope a few bounces in front of the center fielder. It nearly beheaded the base umpire, sending him sprawling to the ground. Merkle took off toward second base. The runner on third could have walked home with the winning tally.

As Doyle would say famously three years later, "It's great to be young and a New York Giant."

At that instant, Fred Merkle was on top of the world.

CUBS INFIELD FEATURING HARRY STEINFELDT,
JOE TINKER, JOHNNY EVERS AND FRANK CHANCE

CAST OF CHARACTERS

THE MAGNIFICENT MORDECAI BROWN
THREW A DEVASTATING CURVE

They're universally recognized today as the "Cubbies," the "lovable losers," a franchise with the longest futility streak in the history of professional sports at 101 years and counting without a World Series title and 64 without even a league pennant. They sell hope and waiting for a next year that never comes.

It wasn't always like this.

The Chicago Cubs of 1906 through 1910 won 530 games and lost only 235 for a .693 winning percentage—the best five-year run in baseball history. They won back-to-back Series crowns and four league pennants. In 1909, they fell short despite a 104-49 record. They were the greatest team of the entire deadball era, arguably the best ever and the antithesis of "cuddly."

Frank Selee, who had managed Boston to five NL titles, assembled the core of what would become the mighty Cubs. He moved Frank Chance from catcher to first base and gave the full-time catching job to the hugely underrated Johnny Kling. He took a chance on alarmingly skinny second baseman Johnny Evers. He shifted Joe Tinker from third base to shortstop. In a trade with the Cardinals, Selee stole ace right-hander Mordecai "Three Finger" Brown.

Seeing a young team on the rise, Chicago sportswriters began to refer to the promising kids as "Cubs," a nickname that stuck.

Selee was unable to finish the job. He contracted tuberculosis and stepped down in the summer of 1905 just when Charles Murphy took over as the new owner. Chicago made a seamless transition as Murphy promoted Chance to player-manager. It was an unusually wise and lucid decision by the erratic Murphy, who eventually alienated just about everyone in baseball, including Chance.

Chance adopted Selee's stern management approach and defly filled the team's remaining holes. He sent aging players to Brooklyn in exchange for talented, young out-fielder Jimmy Sheckard. He added the last infield piece by acquiring solid third baseman Harry Steinfeldt in a trade with Cincinnati.

The 1908 Cubs featured an enviable quartet of start-ing pitchers in Brown, young Ed Reulbach, righty Orval Overall and sidearming lefty Jack Pfiester. They boasted a stellar outfield of Sheckard, Jimmy "the Human Mosqui-to" Slagle and Frank "Wildfire" Schulte as well as a pair of talented utility men in "Circus Solly" Hofman and rookie Heinie Zimmerman.

As special as Brown, Tinker, Evers and Chance were, this was a complete team with quality filling every key roster spot, proficiency in every aspect of the game and a toughness to overcome any obstacles.

Brown was elected posthumously to the Hall of Fame in 1949. Tinker, Evers and Chance were inducted three years earlier. It's unclear if the three were voted in because they were deemed great individually—which is a bit of stretch in each case—or integral to the success of a team that can lay claim to being the best ever. This is one of those juicy baseball debates that never will end.

It's probably not true that the exposure of a poem helped the threesome get into Cooperstown. In 1910, Franklin P. Adams inserted the catchy doggerel into his *New York Evening Mail* column to fill space, but the poem really didn't get widespread exposure until 1947, a year after the trio was admitted to the Hall.

These are the saddest of possible words—
Tinker to Evers to Chance.
Trio of Bear Cubs and fleeter than birds—
Tinker to Evers to Chance.
Thoughtlessly pricking our gonfalon bubble,
Making a Giant hit into a double—
Words that are weighty with nothing but trouble:
Tinker to Evers to Chance.

CUBS' CORNERSTONES

If you had to pick one National League player who personified the deadball era, it would be Johnny "the Crab" Evers.

Evers was 5 foot 9, a wiry but rail-thin 125 pounds. He weighed 20 pounds less when he first came up in 1902. He would spend his entire career pounding down candy bars to keep his weight up. Evers had a protruding jaw, a perpetual smirk, a genuine passion for getting under the skin of opponents and umpires, and an obsession to win.

He was a left-handed hitter who would slap singles, bunt or walk to get on base, steal and find a way to score. Evers was the NL's premier defensive second baseman, forever dodging teeth-clenched base runners. He was loud, annoying, neurotic, combative and fearless.

Hall of Fame umpire Bill Klem, who officiated games for 37 years, called Evers "the toughest and meanest man I ever saw on a ball field."

First baseman Chance barely tolerated Evers' ceaseless high-pitched chatter. He dreamed of dispatching the brilliant second-sacker to the outfield just to get him out of earshot.

Tinker and Evers despised each other and never spoke, except when it was necessary to communicate on the field. The silly feud started in 1905 when, according to Tinker, Evers jumped in a cab and left Tinker and several teammates behind. Two years later, the two were playing catch from close range, and—said Evers—Tinker fired the ball way too fast, breaking Evers' finger.

Evers was so full of nervous energy that Mathewson said he couldn't wear watches because all the electricity in his system would cause them to malfunction. Although that story may have been apocryphal, Evers did miss most of the 1911 season due to a nervous breakdown.

In his last great season, he led the 1914 "Miracle Braves" to a World Series title and earned the Chalmers Award as the NL's MVP. He was maniacal in his role as team captain and also in brief stints as a manager.

Evers supposedly curled up every night in bed studying the rulebook. While that also sounds doubtful, he was definitely obsessed with winning and searching for any little possible edge. He certainly found one in 1908.

Chance, the "Peerless Leader," was the glue that held the contentious Cubs together. He also was known as "Husk" for his imposing 6-0, 190 build. He was fair and universally respected, but he would punch your lights out if you didn't do it his way.

He was a solid righty hitter yet always willing to draw a walk or get hit by a pitch. In an era long before batting helmets, Chance crowded the plate and took a few too many pitches off the noggin. He lost his hearing in one ear and some of it in the other. He developed a blood clot that required brain surgery in 1912, his last season with the Cubs, for whom he compiled a .664 winning percentage as manager in seven-and-a-half seasons.

Chance likely gained entrance to the Hall of Fame more for his achievements as a manager than as a player. Injuries limited him to only six seasons in which he played more than 100 games. In '06, he peaked at 136 games and led the NL with 103 runs scored.

His 1906 team went 116-36 for a .763 winning percentage that still stands as the best for a regular season. To put that in perspective for younger fans, those Cubs were five full games better than the 2001 Mariners (116-46) and seven better than the 1998 Yankees (114-48).

Tinker was the anchor of Chicago's impregnable defense. He led NL shortstops in fielding percentage five times and in range factor four times.

He was a lethal clutch hitter, particularly off Mathewson. Tinker couldn't touch Matty his first two years, but he adjusted by going with a much longer bat, enabling him to reach outside pitches and still get around on the great one's inside offerings. He hit over .400 against Mathewson in 1908 and over .350 for his career. With typical class, Matty tipped his cap to Tinker, acknowledging him as a "thorn in my side" ever since he switched to "that pole."

He was the most durable of the famous Cubs. He also was the most even-tempered, but no less competitive. "If you didn't honestly and furiously hate the Giants, you weren't a real Cub," declared Tinker.

Tinker managed the Chicago Whales of the short-lived Federal League in 1914 and to a pennant in 1915 before managing the Cubs in '16. These were the first years of what would become Wrigley Field, then named Weeghman Park. Charles Weeghman briefly ran the Cubs after owning the Whales.

The odyssey of Brown, the Cubs' three-fingered marvel, began when he was seven years old. Brown stuck his hand in a corn shredder and came out with a stump of an index finger and shortened middle and pinkie fingers. With his mangled hand still in splints, he suffered a fall a few weeks later that caused atrophy and curling of the two smallest digits.

Brown turned the handicap into an advantage, developing a grip that imparted extra spin. His fastball had natural sinking action, and his curveball broke sharply downward just as it reached the plate. Ty Cobb said that Brown's curve was "the most devastating pitch I ever faced."

Escaping the coalmines of Indiana, "Miner" Brown averaged 24 wins in his eight full seasons with the Cubs. His career earned run average of 2.06 is the lowest of anyone who pitched at least 3,000 innings.

MIKE DONLIN SPORTING
WORLD'S CHAMPIONS JERSEY

He won 239 games, started 332 and completed 273. He doubled as an outstanding relief pitcher, saving 49 games. In their legendary head-to-head meetings, Three Finger went 13-10 versus Mathewson. It's inexplicable that Brown, who later managed two teams, wasn't voted into the Hall long before he died.

Chicago entered 1908 as a slight favorite over the Pirates and the rebuilt Giants. The Cubs were in their prime and seeking a third straight league pennant and second consecutive Series title.

New-Look Giants

McGraw wasn't about to sit still after his aging team fell to second place in 1906 and fourth the next year. He took a big risk by luring back talented but wayward "Turkey Mike" Donlin and appointed the slugging right-fielder team captain. He fleeced the Boston Doves in an off-season trade, shedding five fading players and acquiring 24-year-old shortstop Al Bridwell, veteran first baseman Fred Tenney and a decent backup catcher.

The 1908 baseball season was all about theatrical drama. It wouldn't have been the same without the flamboyant 29-year-old Donlin, who strutted like a turkey and sported a scar—from a knifing—on the right cheek of his handsome face. Right in his prime, the colorful playboy kissed off the 1907, 1909 and 1910 seasons to tour vaudeville with his gorgeous actress-wife Mabel

Hite. This was McGraw's third of five go-rounds with his younger alter ego. In the first, Donlin hit .340 for the 1901 Orioles but was released the next spring while serving five months in jail for drunkenly accosting two chorus girls. Agreeing to a no-alcohol clause in his 1908 contract, Donlin hit .334, knocked in 106 runs and played in a team-leading 155 games.

McGraw's other big risk was to go with youngsters in his middle infield. That paid off, too. Shortstop Bridwell and second baseman Doyle were erratic in the field but made up for that by hitting .285 and .308, respectively.

Tenney and incumbent third-sacker Art Devlin were solid at the corners. Rugged Roger Bresnahan excelled at catcher and hit third in the lineup. No one laughed—at least not to his face—when the future Hall of Famer introduced shin guards in 1907. Cy Seymour, considered one of the top center fielders, had a big year at the plate. McGraw purchased Moose McCormick, who hit .292, from the Phillies in early July to upgrade left field and complete a brilliant remake of his lineup.

In his prime at 27, Mathewson had his best year, notching a 37-11 record and 1.43 ERA. He threw 390.2 innings, starting 44 games and finishing 34. Lefty Hooks Wiltse stepped up with his career season, a 23-14 mark and 2.24 ERA. McGraw felt that he had five talented arms behind those two.

"Matty," or "Big Six," was the All-American role model who almost singlehandedly lifted the public perception of ballplayers from louts to idols. Blonde-haired, blue-eyed and a strapping 6 feet 1½ inches, 195 pounds, Mathewson was a three-sport star, honors student and class president at Bucknell University. After his amazing three-shutout performance in the 1905 Series, Mathewson became a national sensation, endorsing countless products. Matty influenced the persona of enormously popular fictional sports hero Frank Merriwell.

He was one of many players who considered Sunday a holy day and refused to play on the Sabbath. But Mathewson was not quite as squeaky-clean as his image. He liked the occasional drink and cigar and was told frequently by McGraw to stop winning so much money from his teammates at the poker table.

Mathewson, who would die too young at age 45 of tuberculosis, finished his career with a 373–188 record, 2.13 ERA and a staggering 4,783 innings. In his book, *Pitching in a Pinch,* he freely shared the secrets of his success. He paced himself and saved his best stuff for key moments, articulating the approach required for all starting pitchers, who were expected to finish what they started regardless of their pitch counts. He described his best pitch, the "fade-away," later known as a screwball, which broke sharply down and away from a left-handed hitter.

Bill James, in his *Historical Baseball Abstract,* said he admired Mathewson for his guts more than anything else:

"Mathewson was one of the very few men, and maybe the only one in baseball, who would say at the time that he thought the White Sox were throwing the 1919 World Series. He was the one who tried to have Hal Chase thrown out of baseball before the World Series was fixed."

Odd Couple

Mathewson and McGraw made for the strangest of bedfellows. The dictatorial McGraw, dubbed "Little Napoleon" or "Muggsy" (which he hated), made his own rules on and off the field.

"McGraw eats gunpowder every morning for breakfast and washes it down with warm blood," cracked Giants' coach Arlie Latham.

He co-owned a pool hall in Manhattan with notorious bookmaker Arnold Rothstein, the architect of the thrown 1919 Series that nearly ruined baseball. He committed perjury by falsely claiming he didn't offer a contract to bring back Chase—baseball's most outrageously crooked player—to the Giants for the 1920 season. He was arrested during spring training of 1904 for illegal betting and resisting arrest. He bet $400 on the Giants to win the 1905 Series, directly violating a no-gambling league edict.

In 1905, McGraw waged a baseless smear campaign against amiable Pittsburgh owner Barney Dreyfuss. In 1906, McGraw—furious about a bad call and ejection by umpire Jim Johnstone in a loss to the Cubs—refused to let the ump into the park the next day. In 1908, he insulted Boston first baseman Dan McGann and wound up fighting the former Giant in the lobby of the swank Copley Square Hotel.

Through it all, the hard-drinking McGraw never got more than a 20-game suspension as a National League manager. Several factors protected him. He had become a celebrity in and outside of the sport. Baseball had developed a pattern of turning a blind eye to its gambling problem. NL president Harry Pulliam consistently shied away from controversy and tough decisions. Brush was one of the most powerful owners and consistently backed McGraw.

Like most tormented souls, McGraw wasn't all bad. He made loans to ballplayers, knowing he'd never see the money again. He was generous to charities. As a baseball manager, he was an innovator and a shrewd team-builder and in-game strategist.

Mostly, McGraw needed to win, and he thought he would in 1908. Leaving no stone unturned, he even added a full-time physician to Brush's payroll by hiring Dr. Joseph Creamer for $2,800.

Wagner's Pirates

The official spelling of *Pittsburgh* lacked the *h* from 1890 to 1911. No problem. As the 1908 season began, the city also was missing Honus Wagner, its superstar shortstop. Big problem.

"The Flying Dutchman" was the best player of the era and possibly the greatest ever. He just didn't look like

HONUS "THE FLYING DUTCHMAN" WAGNER

it. He was a large man with doleful eyes who moved un-gracefully on extremely bowed legs.

The Pirates weren't built like the quality-deep Cubs. They had to have the 34-year-old Wagner, who was a holdout. He claimed he was tired. Dreyfuss, recognizing his star was underpaid, doubled his salary to 10 grand. Wagner, finding enough energy to play 10 more seasons, returned for the fourth game.

With Wagner, a good team was a great team again. Player-manager Fred Clarke was a tough-minded leader in the mold of Chance and McGraw, an excellent left field-er and a future Hall of Famer. He had a superb pitching

staff led by Cooperstown-bound Vic Willis, a terrific third
baseman in "Wee" Tommy Leach and several other good
players. The negatives were meager hitting from the cen-
ter-field and first-base positions. Clarke tolerated a third
offensive sinkhole because of catcher George Gibson's
gifts as a defender and leader.

Wagner had one of his greatest seasons, leading the NL
in batting average (.354), on-base percentage (.415), slugging
(.542), runs batted in (109), hits (201), doubles (39), triples
(19), stolen bases (53) and putouts (354). His 10 homers left
him two shy of the home-run title and Triple Crown.

The next year, American Tobacco Company halted
the press run of its T206 baseball card featuring Wagner
because he refused to grant permission. He said he did not
want to be associated with a product promoting cigarettes
to children. That seemed a peculiar stance for a tobacco
chewer who had appeared in such cards and ads before.
He may have wanted more money. Wagner was neither
greedy nor financially savvy, but he understood the value
of his name. He was the first player, in 1905, to put his
autograph on Louisville Slugger bats.

Regardless, the card became the most valuable of all.
Fewer than 200 of the cards ever reached the public. One
of them was sold in 2007 to a collector in California for
$2.8 million.

Wagner led proud Pirate teams that won the decade's
first three NL pennants and a fourth in 1909. In 1908,
however, the Pittsburgh franchise had issues beyond the

abilities of its players. Attendance flagged because the city's industrial base was slow to recover from the previous year's recession.

Dreyfuss already had given up on old and wet Exposition Field. He announced in March the construction of Forbes Field. The steel-and-concrete marvel would open in June of 1909, two months after the debut of Philadelphia's equally glorious Shibe Park.

The owner, weary of all the costly postponements at soggy Exposition, introduced baseball's first infield tarp early in 1908. The Pirates, however, preferred the road, compiling an amazing 56–21 record away from home.

The Pirates flew under the radar compared to the surly, big-market Giants and Cubs, but they went 23–21 against their two rivals in 1908.

Pittsburgh won a famously disputed game with eerie implications against the Cubs on September 4. Exactly a month later, the Pirates were in a position to clinch the pennant with one more victory—on the road at Chicago.

Philadelphia, a good fourth-place team, was a potential spoiler because of its dominant pitching staff, which had a chance to get even stronger if 22-year-old southpaw Harry Coveleski proved ready for the big time.

The NL's second division was composed of Cincinnati—which had good pitching but abominable hitting—and the hapless trio of Boston, Brooklyn and St. Louis. The Cubs would go 69–19 against that foursome, to the Pirates' 62-26 and the Giants' 60–28.

Pulliam was starting his sixth year as National League president. A rather stiff Kentucky gentleman, he had been a practicing attorney, sportswriter and state congressman before moving up the ladder to president of Dreyfuss's Louisville and Pittsburgh franchises. He was a compromise choice to take over as the NL's top dog in December 1902. Pulliam was a conciliatory rather than take-charge leader. The pressures on him mounted as baseball grew in popularity each year. The Giants were his nemesis. McGraw constantly tested his authority. Brush disliked Pulliam so much that he wouldn't even give his own league president a free admission pass to the Polo Grounds.

Hank O'Day, once a big-league pitcher and 22-game winner, entered his 14th of 35 seasons as a major-league umpire. He later had brief stints as manager of the Cubs and Reds, earning the distinction as the only man in history to play, manage and umpire in the National League. He was considered honest, dedicated, extremely knowledgeable about the rules and an excellent game-caller. Taciturn, aloof and antisocial, he had the personality of a tree stump. O'Day never married and lived with his sister. He rarely spoke to fellow umpire and former pitcher Bob Emslie, his closest friend in baseball. O'Day preferred to work games by himself. If questioned about a play, he would provide a basic explanation and say nothing further.

Pulliam and O'Day had no idea what would hit them late in the 1908 season.

NATIONAL BASEBALL COMMISSION: HARRY PULLIAM (PRESIDENT, NATIONAL
LEAGUE), GARRY HERRMANN (OWNER, CINCINNATI REDS AND PRESIDENT
OF THE COMMISSION), BAN JOHNSON (PRESIDENT, AMERICAN LEAGUE),
JOHN E. BRUCE (SECRETARY OF THE COMMISSION). NOTE THAT PULLIAM IS
CLEARLY DECLINING IN HEALTH.

BARRELING
INTO SEPTEMBER

UMPIRE HANK O'DAY

The play on the field was as brilliant in 1908 as the leadership off the field was poor. Baseball executives met at New York's Waldorf Astoria in February for their annual preseason meetings and whiffed on virtually every item they discussed.

Johnson stated that his American League would be vigilant against gambling. It wasn't. With a straight face, Pulliam insisted that the problem no longer existed in his National League. During the season, he repeated that claim shortly after a bookmaker approached him in the middle of a game. He walked away instead of having the bookie expelled from the park.

The rowdy behavior of fan rooter clubs had gotten out of hand. The executives debated several crowd-control remedies and finally dropped the matter altogether, presumably not wanting to alienate their most ardent paying customers. The owners also considered—but ultimately passed on—banning glass bottles after Chance and an umpire had been seriously injured by the thrown objects the previous year.

The sport had grown too fast and complex for games to be covered by one umpire, who couldn't see all the action—and dirty tricks—taking place behind him. To their credit, the leagues recognized this and began assigning both a home-plate and base ump to more games. But they didn't train or hire enough new officials. Fewer than half the games—41 percent in the NL—would be called by two umpires in 1908. The criteria used to determine which games would be allocated two umps were subjective and flawed. The important September 4th contest between the Cubs and Pirates was one of the games that should have been double-covered but wasn't.

Weather delays and postponements were an ongoing problem. Johnson declared, wisely, that resumption of delayed games would be left up to the umpires. Pulliam decided, unwisely, that both managers would have to agree. Predictably, the manager of the trailing team never favored resumption if the game wasn't yet official. He wanted a postponement and a full make-up game later. Just as obviously, the manager of the leading team never wanted the game to continue if it was official. He wanted the abbreviated victory in the books. Pulliam's decision led to more postponements, thus more late-season make-up games.

Pulliam got one thing right by mandating that every NL team must play all 154 of its games if any of the remaining contests had a bearing on the pennant race. Johnson blew it by stating that, in the event of any unplayed games, the final standings would be determined by the teams' winning percentages.

In terms of being proactive, Johnson had it all over Pulliam. Once the season got underway, Johnson would continue his practice of reviewing game situations involving rules and determining how they would be called in the future. With tragic consequences, Pulliam simply kept rubber-stamping whatever his umps called, with no further explanation or clarification.

The fans, no more sophisticated in their role than baseball's naïve leaders were in theirs, weren't too concerned with administrative items. It was finally mid-April and time to play ball!

Hornet Nests

At the outset, Chicago and retooled New York each won five of six games on the road while Pittsburgh, with Wagner getting back into playing shape, went 3–3.

The Cubs prevailed 1–0 April 17 at Cincinnati's raucous Palace of the Fans to complete a season-opening three-game sweep. As was their custom, the rabid fans of "Rooter's Row" sat close to the action, swilled cheap beer and taunted home and visiting players alike. Police had to whisk Reds' standout third baseman Hans Lobert off the field after repeated skirmishes, including an accusation by one of the most obnoxious spectators that Lobert spat in his face. It wasn't as if Lobert couldn't take a joke. He once raced a horse around the bases and agreed with everyone that he lost "by a nose," his being the most prominent in baseball.

Moving on to St. Louis the next day, the Cubs lost their only game of the week, a 3–2 defeat that infuriated Evers. This was one of 87 games O'Day called by himself versus only 51 with a partner. The game was tied 2–2 in the bottom of the ninth with men on first and third and one out. The batter hit a hard grounder to Evers. The canny Cub froze the man on third with a glance, tagged the runner approaching him and tried to run toward first base to complete the double play. The runner thwarted Evers by tripping him, but O'Day—watching the man coming home from third—didn't see that. Evers blamed not O'Day but the staffing of just one umpire.

Exhibiting his flair for the dramatic, Donlin made the Giants' home opener April 22 a day to remember for the record Polo Grounds crowd of more than 25,000. Down to his last strike, Turkey Mike lashed a two-run homer over the right-field fence with two outs in the bottom of the ninth to give New York a 3–2 victory over Brooklyn.

Mabel Hite wept with joy from her private suite and then worried for her husband's safety as Giants' fans mobbed their hero and tried to tear off his uniform. The *New York Journal* said the crowd "went clean crazy."

The *Chicago Tribune* complained about a play earlier in the ninth inning of the Giants' game. Rookie Fred Merkle, pinch-hitting for Mathewson, lofted what appeared to be a catchable fly ball to right field. The Brooklyn right fielder retreated into a beehive of Giants' fans. The ball fell safely, and Merkle was given a ground-rule double. He advanced to third on a sacrifice bunt.

Few accounts of the game related what happened next. Tenney hit an infield grounder, and Merkle was out after getting caught between third and home. Donlin's game-winning clout took the kid off the hook.

Donlin would finish the season with six home runs, tied with Tinker for fourth most in the National League. The Giants hit 20 round-trippers, third in the NL. Philadelphia led the AL with 21 four-baggers. The Chicago White Sox hit only three homers, all in July. Most of the year's 267 homers (about a nine-day total now) were hit inside the park.

The Giants improved to 6–1 but then began to blow games to inferior opponents with bad base-running, mental and physical miscues and spotty pitching depth after Mathewson and Wiltse. Joe "Iron Man" McGinnity, 37, was no longer effective as a starter. An ugly 7–6 road loss to the hapless Boston Doves April 29 precipitated McGraw's hotel brawl with McGann.

On the same day, the visiting White Sox downed the slumping Tigers 6–3. Sox player-manager Fielder Jones called for a suicide squeeze bunt. With his foot on the rubber, Detroit's pitcher made a rushed throw to the plate. The catcher jumped in front of the plate to snag the toss, making it impossible for the Chicago batter to bunt the ball. Umpire Silk O'Loughlin upheld the play. Jones, a stickler for the rules, criticized the call but could not file a formal protest because his team won the game.

AL president Johnson studied the matter and overruled his umpire. He said the pitcher was subject to a balk call if he hurried his motion while on the rubber. If it was a legal pitch, the catcher could not step up and get in the way of the batter's attempt at the ball. If the pitcher stepped off the rubber (before starting his windup) and threw, it was a nonpitch, allowing the catcher to move up legally. Perfect. Unfortunately, this was not the way the NL's Pulliam operated. He had several opportunities to clarify how certain plays should be ruled but continued his practice of supporting his umpires' calls and going no further.

EARLY STRUGGLES

Even great teams encounter rough patches over the course of a long season. The Giants and Pirates got theirs out of the way early. New York slipped to 14–15, sixth place and five-and-a-half games behind the Cubs after a double-header loss at St. Louis on May 23. Pittsburgh sat in fifth place, four games out, with a 15–15 mark May 29 following a 3–8 skid at home against NL lightweights.

The Cubs (32–20) led for the first nine weeks but looked vulnerable. They went 27–8 versus the league's also-rans but a lame 5–12 against New York and Pittsburgh. This wasn't going to be a cakewalk like the last two years. One issue after another sullied Chicago's mood.

Brown, tending to his ill mother and sister back in Indiana, didn't make his first start until May 3. He left the team again in June upon the passing of his mother. His sister died a month later. Former pitching stalwarts Carl Lundgren and Chick Fraser faltered, forcing Chance to rely heavily on Brown, Reulbach, Overall and Pfiester for the duration. Chance, Evers, Kling and all three starting outfielders wound up missing an average of 40 games due to injuries.

Although the public didn't learn about it till later, the cranky Cubs imploded in their clubhouse June 2 after the Pirates and Wagner bombed them for the third straight game.

Sheckard, the highly respected veteran left fielder, said something to Zimmerman that offended the brash rookie. Zimmerman hit Sheckard on the forehead with an ammonia bottle, which broke on contact. The fluid seeped into Sheckard's eyes, nearly blinding him and causing him to miss 39 games. Zimmerman then tussled with Chance, which was a very bad idea. Several Cubs joined in and pounded the rookie, disabling him for a couple of weeks. Chicago didn't need any more injuries, especially self-inflicted. This episode set the tone for Zimmerman's wildly uneven career. He won the Triple Crown in 1912 and then, as a member of McGraw's Giants, got banned from baseball for playing a role in throwing the 1919 World Series.

By the end of June, the Pirates—despite getting no hitting punch from three positions—had vaulted to the top spot with a 40–22 record after a blistering 25–7 turnabout. The fractious Cubs (37–23) were a game back, the Giants (37–27) three behind.

Chicago was a rollicking town in 1908. Its baseball fans treated every game like a festival, but they were considered respectful. They witnessed a bit of everything in a four-game split with the Giants in mid-July at West Side Grounds.

Brown sported a 13–1 record despite his bereavement absences and heavy heart. He started the opener and didn't even make it out of the fourth inning in an 11–0 Giants shellacking.

The next day, McGraw summoned Mathewson from the clubhouse in the ninth inning. The Giants led 4–1, but the Cubs threatened with the bases loaded and one out. Matty, thinking the game was well in hand without him, had decided to take a shower. An exasperated McGraw was forced to insert a different reliever, who promptly gave up a run-scoring hit. Finally, Matty's teammates reached the dripping wet Giants' ace, who hastily threw on most of his uniform and saved the game in his street shoes.

The third game lived up to its huge billing. Brown sought his seventh consecutive victory over Mathewson and got it with a 1–0 shutout masterpiece. After making two sterling defensive plays, Tinker stepped to the plate against Matty in the fourth inning and belted an inside-the-park homer to center. Cy Seymour tried to cut off the ball before it rolled past him toward the 560-foot wall marker. Tinker navigated quite the obstacle course. Third baseman Devlin, in true McGraw style, attempted an elbow block. Zimmerman, coaching third, put on the stop sign by grabbing Tinker, who ran right over him.

Tragedy accompanied Tinker's heroics. William Hudson, 14, watched with excitement from the roof of an apartment building. Apparently leaning over for a better view, the boy fell 50 feet to his death.

In the series finale, southpaw Pfiester relieved control-plagued Reulbach and hurled seven frames of one-run ball to give the Cubs—trailing 4–3—a chance in the bottom of the ninth. After an Evers walk and Pat Moran double, Tinker torpedoed the New Yorkers again with a two-run double off a tiring Wiltse for the victory. McGraw, fuming, slugged a kid on his way to the clubhouse.

At the season's midpoint, the Pirates (48–33), Giants (47–33) and Cubs (46–33) were within a mere game of each other and deadlocked in the loss column. Only three games separated Detroit (48–33), St. Louis (46–35), Cleveland (45–35) and the White Sox (45–36) atop the AL standings.

Shenanigans

The Giants took a hostile disposition with them from Chicago to St. Louis. In the series opener against the Cardinals, Donlin charged in from the outfield three times to chase and insult umpire Johnstone. Not surprisingly, the Giants led all teams with 20 ejections—McGraw's seven the most among managers, Donlin's six pacing all players.

Before the last scheduled game in St. Louis, McGraw abruptly took his battered team and vamoosed to New York to rest up for a big four-game series against the Pirates. This was not an uncommon maneuver for a beat-up contender. Play the game later when your team is likely to be healthier. Even the Giants-fawning New York press criticized McGraw for the chicanery, but Pulliam let it go and rescheduled the game.

Chance pulled off a similar ploy July 5. The Pirates visited Chicago with the expectation of playing a well-advertised doubleheader. One of the games was a make-up. The shorthanded Cubs were drubbed 10–5 in the opener and simply refused to play the second contest. Pittsburgh protested, Johnstone ruled a forfeit and Pulliam—for once overruling one of his umpires—denied the forfeit because he said the league had not received formal notice of the plan to play a pair. The result was more schedule manipulation.

Two things became apparent when the now-rested Giants returned home Friday, July 24 to take on the Pirates. Their rabid fans had multiplied, and the Polo Grounds desperately needed more seats and security. As scalpers flourished outside the park, a new wave of bookmakers prospered inside. More bookies drifted from the racetrack to the ballpark because of a new state law against gambling on the ponies.

Rent-a-cops did their best to handle the record throng of 34,000, nearly double the park's capacity. It was the police commissioner's policy to station officers outside the park but not on the inside. Let the Giants deal with their crowds. With standing room space filled, fans flooded the outfield as close as medium-depth range and completely filled foul territory. They stood in front of the dugouts, forcing the players of both teams to sit along the sidelines.

Numerous fans dashed across the field to celebrate Giants rallies, including one particular idiot who turned handsprings. No one was ejected. Somehow, two teams played a baseball game, Matty losing 7–2 and Wagner—nearly getting stripped by the throng afterward—going 5-for-5.

Brush didn't do a whole lot about security, but he quickly remodeled the park in late August, boosting capacity to about 28,000 by lengthening the grandstands and adding bleacher seating and a fence across the entire outfield. With McGraw in desperate need of mound depth,

Brush also funded the then-outlandish sum of $11,000 to sign southpaw phenom Rube Marquard, who would become one of the year's most publicized flops.

Beginning August in a funk, the Cubs lost two in a row to the host Giants and were in dire need of a win on the 11th. Pfiester furnished it with a 4–0 shutout gem. But the Phillies, no pushovers, extended the battered Bruins' woes by winning a pair. Chicago, now 2–7 for the month, fell to 58–45, six games behind the Pirates (64–39) and three shy of the Giants (61–42).

Welcoming back their walking wounded, the Cubs rebounded with a 9–2 run against noncontenders just before the Giants made their final trip to the Windy City for a three-game set August 27–30. Thus far, Chicago was an unacceptable 3–5 versus New York at home and 5–10 overall.

Fan-tastic

With both of its teams battling for pennants, Chicago had gone as baseball-daffy as New York. For those folks who could not attend the games, the new rage was to watch simulated action on electronic scoreboards. The board operators received the game information by telegraph, lit the bulbs corresponding to each player and re-created every pitch and base advance. With no radio or television in those days, the fans were hooked immediately. The storefront boards attracted crowds that often spilled into the streets and blocked traffic. The bigger games were shown in major indoor venues such as Chicago's Orchestra Hall and New York's Madison Square Garden. The proprietors sold hot dogs—only recently a baseball staple—and other refreshments.

West Side Grounds was packed to the rafters on Thursday the 27th, but there were also tens of thousands of fans in Chicago and New York glued to the boards. Those stuck in their offices anxiously awaited updates from messenger boys.

Pfiester outdueled Wiltse 5–1. The Cubs' lefty deserved a little baseball luck after a rash of early-season heartbreakers. He got some in the eighth inning. With the bases loaded and one out, Devlin tried to get out of the way of a curveball and popped up to the pitcher to start an easy double play.

By design, Cubs' officials scheduled Friday as an off day to make big-revenue killings Saturday and Sunday. The "blue laws" forbidding baseball games on the Sabbath applied in all cities except Chicago, St. Louis and Cincinnati.

The owners, well aware of most folks' weekday work schedules, abhorred the Sunday ban for financial reasons. Cincinnati owner Garry Herrmann was notably progressive in exposing the sport to more people He announced in August a plan to set up lights at the Palace and host a night game. Nearly 5,000 fans turned out to watch a semipro game under the lights in June of 1909.

The experiment was a success, but baseball's hierarchy wasn't ready for such a radical change. Despite the prospect of windfall profits, there would be no night baseball in the majors until 1935, appropriately, in Cincinnati.

Chicago was abuzz with anticipation for another Brown–Mathewson matchup on Saturday. It took a no-hitter by Mathewson the last time he had beaten the Cubs' ace back in June 1905. Brown prevailed once again, 3–2. Hofman's leadoff double in the fourth ignited a three-run, five-hit rally.

Circus Solly Hofman was an invaluable utility man for the 1908 Cubs, similar to Mark DeRosa exactly 100 years later. Playing in 120 games, Hofman ably filled in at several positions for injured regulars and scored or drove in 97 runs. When he requested a few days off in September to get married, Chance absolutely forbade it until the season ended.

In contrast, Ty Cobb didn't ask. He suddenly bolted the Tigers on August 3 in the heat of the AL pennant race to get hitched and didn't return until five days later. His own teammates viewed Cobb as surly, sullen and now selfish. During the season, he continued to attack blacks over perceived slights. Cobb was arrested for assaulting a black street laborer and kicked a black maid in the stomach. People learned to watch from a safe distance as Cobb won the second of 9 straight batting titles and 12 in all.

The vibe was far more pleasant back in Chicago for Sunday's finale. Pfiester, working on two days' rest, stifled the Giants 2–1 for a fourth straight time to give the Cubs the sweep. Evers and Tinker turned a tough chance into a ballet-like double play to end the New Yorkers' lone threat. Giddy fans celebrated for 15 minutes by throwing cushions and wrecking Merry Widow hats. The Chicago press coined Pfiester "Jack the Giant Killer."

August ended the next day with the Cubs (70–47) a half-game behind the Pirates (71–47) and Giants (69–45). Four AL teams were separated by three-and a-half games.

Could the last quarter of the season possibly be any better? Oh, yes.

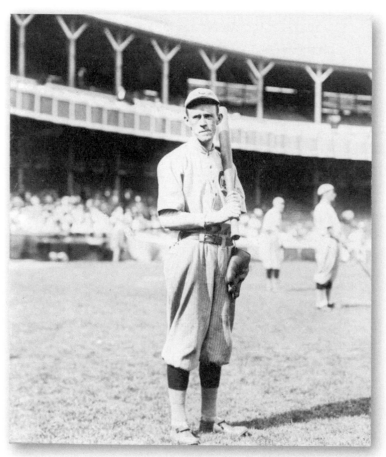

Johnny "The Crab" Evers

GILL, YOU'RE NOT "IT"

THE UNFORTUNATE FRED MERKLE

Future Hall of Famers Brown and Vic Willis hurled nine and a half innings of shutout ball September 4 at Pittsburgh. The stakes were high. The Cubs and Pirates were in a virtual tie for second place, one game behind the Giants.

The man in question on the game's final play easily could have gone down in history as Warren "Bonehead" Gill. That would have been unjust. As it turned out, fate spared him and chose Merkle, which was just as wrong.

Gill was one of the hundreds upon hundreds of marginal players who got a brief taste of the majors and then disappeared forever. The 29-year-old first baseman hit .224 in 76 at-bats and 27 games during his only season in the big leagues. Clarke tried Gill and three other suspects at the position, and every one of them was terrible.

Clarke singled to lead off the bottom of the 10th. He advanced to second on Leach's sacrifice and to third on Wagner's single. Brown plunked Gill to load the bases but fanned the next batter for the second out. Chief Wilson lined Brown's first pitch to center for a clean single, and Clarke trotted home with the game's lone—and winning—run.

Gill did what players always had done in that situation. He broke off his run between first and second base and high-tailed it to the clubhouse to avoid the onrushing crowd.

Technically, this was a no-no. Rule 59 stated that a run shall not count if a runner reached home "on or during a play in which the third man be forced out or be put out before reaching first base."

In other words, going strictly by the rule, the runner should proceed to, and touch, second base. If he didn't, a fielder with the ball could touch the bag first for a force-out and the inning's third out, which would negate the run.

Except that the rule always had been treated as completely irrelevant in that situation. Umpires hustled off the field right along with the players. Game over. Get the heck outta there before the drunken fans converged. On an obvious game-winning hit to the outfield, the umps assumed a base runner's advance to the next base. Custom always had trumped the rule on that play, the spirit of the law prevailing over the letter of the law.

Of course, if someone had forewarned Gill that Rule 59 suddenly would apply on that play and supersede tradition for the first time ever in baseball history, it's reasonable to believe he would have trotted a few more steps and placed his foot on the bag. No one told him, so he didn't.

Manager Clarke was a very astute baseball man, his Pirates a heady, alert bunch. None of them yelled out to Gill to go all the way to second base. Why would they? They would have peeled off, too. It was universal baseball practice.

Evers Tests the Water

The rule never had been tested before. Naturally, it was Evers who tried. He called for the ball, stepped on second base and appealed to umpire O'Day to call Gill out, which would disallow the run and keep the score 0–0.

In the typical scene, the losing team immediately walked off the field, heads down. None of the Cubs budged from their positions. They obviously had prepped themselves for this situation.

Evers may have gotten the idea from the Sunday, July 19th edition of the *Chicago Tribune*. The paper ran a weekly Q & A column entitled "Inquisitive Fans." A fan asked if the run from third would count if the batter stopped running between home and first after hitting safely to the outfield in a tie game with two outs in the bottom of the ninth. "No. Runner cannot score when third out is made before reaching first base," replied the Trib, invoking Rule 59.

Nobody knows if the column prompted Evers, but it's an extremely plausible theory—first raised by G. H. Fleming, author of *The Unforgettable Season.*

The piece ran in Chicago's most popular newspaper. Evers was more obsessed than anyone with winning, rules and reading about the rules. Just six weeks later, a Rule 59 scenario presented itself in a crucial situation. It cost Evers and the Cubs absolutely nothing to test the waters, and the obvious upside was that it might prevent a costly loss. Smart move.

O'Day, allowed to work one of the season's most important games by himself, refused to call Gill out because he said he didn't see the play. As he stated later, he was looking to see if Clarke touched home plate. If there had been two umpires that day, the base ump would have seen Gill veer off and possibly upheld the Cubs' plea for the force-out.

Cubs' owner Murphy filed a formal protest, then promptly took the steam right out of it by commenting, "I do not expect the protest will be allowed, but it is certainly just, and should prove a strong argument for the double-umpire system."

Only the Chicago and Pittsburgh newspapers reported on the play the next day. The Giants were in Philadelphia. On Sunday the 6th, an editorial in the *Pittsburgh Post* read: "the final play of Friday's game between the Cubs and the Pirates doesn't come often, but next time it happens it is safe to predict that none who took part in the game will overlook the importance of touching the next base."

The protest resulted in articles by the national publications. *The Sporting Life* correctly predicted that Pulliam would stand on precedent and disallow the protest. *The Sporting News* criticized Murphy for bothering with a mere technicality. In McGraw's own backyard, the *New York Globe* debated the matter.

Even that last wave of coverage escaped the attention of the Giants and the detail-minded McGraw. Legendary sportswriter Fred Lieb called it one of baseball's most enduring mysteries.

MISSED OPPORTUNITIES

No one on New York informed its 19-year-old rookie only 19 days after the Gill game to advance to the next base instead of adhering to baseball tradition. Merkle, already considered one of the Giants' smartest players, would not have needed more than a brief heads-up.

With Evers successfully planting the seed, O'Day was ready to reverse baseball tradition and call the play

differently the next time it came up. He would be allowed to keep that as his little secret. On a protest, Pulliam only required of his umpires to submit a brief account of a play. The policy perfectly suited the reticent
O'Day. He described the Gill play, said he didn't see it,
and that was it.

The Gill matter presented Pulliam with a golden opportunity to clarify how such a play would be called in the
future. There's no doubt that the proactive Johnson would
have done so if the situation had arisen in an American
League game.

In disallowing the protest a full five days later, Pulliam said the decision belonged "solely to the umpire. The
umpire, in this case, by allowing the winning run ruled
that there was no force at second, because if there had
been the run could not have been scored."

Sigh. The Cubs did execute a force-out. The proper
response would have been to deny the protest because the
lone official did not see the play and justifiably would not
call what he hadn't seen.

With that, Pulliam should have consulted with his fellow authorities and determined how the play would be
called henceforth. Go ahead, by tradition, and keep peel-
ing off to the clubhouse on a game-winning hit? Or alert
everyone to touch the next base because the rulebook
would apply from now on?

"Pulliam's inaction regarding the Gill play was the
equivalent of lighting a fuse to a bomb," said David

W. Anderson, who wrote the factually comprehensive *More Than Merkle.*

A highly critical Bill James wrote, "It is in principle most dangerous to have rules on the books which are not enforced, or have one set of rules written down and another acted out."

Not So Fast, Giants

The Giants, more than recovering from their late August comedown in Chicago, launched September by going on a torrid 18–1 tear.

On the 18th, New York blew the doors off visiting Pittsburgh in a twinbill behind Matty and Wiltse. Donlin was allowed to continue to play in the first game after punching a fan in the eye.

New York (87–46) opened up a four and a half game lead over Chicago (85–53) and five over Pittsburgh (85–54). Even back then, baseball observers looked at the loss column, where this particular margin was huge. The Cubs and Pirates might keep winning, but they couldn't take away the defeats already on their ledgers. They needed Giants' losses—lots of 'em.

The New Yorkers started talking smack. "I can't see how we can lose unless we all drop dead," said pitcher Red Ames. "We will walk in," crowed outfielder Cy Seymour. "I can't help thinking we are sure to win…," added young Merkle.

The resilient Pirates bounced back to take the series' last two games, 6–2 and 2–1. In the September 21 finale, Pittsburgh ace Willis beat a nearly as efficient Mathewson in a brisk one hour and 19 minutes. By all accounts, O'Day blew a call in which a Pirate batter was thrown out by several feet on a grounder to short right field.

On the same day, the visiting Cubs swept a doubleheader from the troublesome Phillies while resting their four best pitchers. Rube Kroh was effective in one of his only two appearances the entire season. Andy Coakley, a solid hurler acquired from the Reds for the stretch run, improved to 2–0 for Chicago.

The Cubs rolled into the Big Apple on the 22nd for another doubleheader to open a gigantic four-game series. With Matty used up and Wiltse needing rest, McGraw had to go with Red Ames and struggling rookie Doc Crandall.

Chicago captured a 4–3, 3–1 sweep. Brown relieved Overall in the seventh inning of the opener. He allowed a two-run single and then shut the door. His arm already warm, Brown made his scheduled start in the second game and went all the way, whiffing Merkle to wiggle out of a late jam.

Doyle, who had been red-hot, was out indefinitely with a severely sprained ankle. Bridwell and Tenney were slumping. Earlier in September, New York covered up its lack of pitching depth by pounding the ball. Now, runs were getting harder to come by.

Because of the rash of make-up games, every team faced a brutally heavy September-October schedule. The Cubs and Pirates had plowed through the worst of theirs. Chicago would play 11 games in 12 days and Pittsburgh 12 in 12, each finishing October 4 with a make-up game against each other. The Giants' slate called for a demanding 17 games in 15 days, including three make-ups with Boston October 5–7.

The Cubs (90–53) had erased their entire four-and-a-half-game deficit in just four days, drawing even with the Giants (87–50), whose smirks were gone after dropping four in a row. The Pirates (88–54) were back in the hunt, only a game and a half back.

Baseball hysteria rose to a whole new level. Tomorrow's Giants–Cubs tilt—Matty versus Jack the Giant Killer—at the asylum known as the Polo Grounds had the feel of a deciding World Series game.

GENTLEMAN CHRISTY MATHEWSON

"MERKLE, YOU
GO PLAY HELL TODAY"

FRED MERKLE READY AT BAT

The irony of baseball's most famous and controversial game—played on September 23, 1908—is that neither team won it that day.

Veteran first baseman Tenney—his lower torso racked by lumbago—started every game of the season except this one. It was only Merkle's second start and first at first base. He began with the line-drive snag to rob Tinker, who was bidding for his fourth game-winning hit of the season against the Giants and third off Mathewson.

Tinker came up again in the top of the fifth inning and laced a liner to right-center. Donlin, slowed by a charley horse, awkwardly tried to stop the ball with his foot. The orb rolled forever, and Tinker circled the bases for a home run, the first one Matty had allowed to anyone since Tinker's back on July 17.

Donlin redeemed himself in the sixth with a run-scoring single to tie the game. That followed an infield hit by Buck Herzog, who was playing second base for the injured Doyle. Herzog had moved to second on a throwing error and to third on Bresnahan's sacrifice.

The inning ended with no further damage, except to base umpire Emslie's pride. Running to second during the third out, Donlin bumped into the official, whose bad toupee was knocked askew, sending the crowd of 20,000—unprecedented for a Wednesday afternoon—into hysterical laughter.

Emslie was considered an excellent ump on the bases, but he took a lot of abuse, especially from McGraw, whose nickname for Emslie was "Wig." After this game, McGraw started calling him "Blind Bob." Emslie put an end to that. One day, he suddenly showed up at a Giants' practice with a rifle, put a dime on the pitching mound, nailed it from home plate and walked away.

Brilliant pitching by Mathewson and Pfiester kept the game at 1–1 and increasingly tense the rest of the way. It was revealed later that Pfiester was throwing with a dislocated tendon in his pitching elbow. "He could not bend his arm, and to pitch a curve brought agony," recalled Evers, who said the pitcher threw only three curveballs the entire game, all saved for Donlin in clutch situations.

After the game, Pfiester went to Youngstown, Ohio, to get treatment from "Bonesetter" Reese, the unofficial—and unlicensed—physician of ballplayers for two decades. Reese felt around with his fingers and moved the tendon back into place, a procedure that would be laughed at today. Nowadays, Pfiester would undergo "Tommy John" or more extensive surgery immediately and miss at least 12 months. His courageous performance in this game got lost in the ensuing controversy.

Matty, facing only 29 batters to get 27 outs, retired the Cubs in order in the top of the ninth.

Crunch Time

With one out in the bottom of the ninth, Devlin singled for only the Giants' fifth hit off Pfiester but was forced out on Moose McCormick's grounder. Devlin slid at Tinker with spikes predictably high, tempers fraying on both sides.

Merkle roped his long single to right, not far from the foul line. He said later he easily could have stretched it into a double, but it was not worth the risk. Schulte had a cannon for an arm, there were two outs, the Giants needed only one run and McCormick easily lumbered around to third base.

The speedy youngster—on top of the world at this point—took a sizable lead off first base. Merkle was unlikely to steal because he had yet to swipe his first big-league bag. He may have been trying to rattle Pfiester and induce a wild pickoff throw. He may have wanted to shorten his run to second and make an infielder fielding a grounder throw to first, eliminating a force at second.

The batter, Bridwell, didn't like whatever Merkle might have been considering. The Giants' shortstop gave his teammate a cautionary furl of the eyebrows. The kid got the message and inched closer to the bag.

Bridwell rocketed Pfiester's first-pitch fastball on a low trajectory just to the right of second base. The screaming liner targeted Emslie, positioned on the grass just past the infield. Not having a good day, Emslie evaded the missile and fell right on his keister.

Moose easily waddled home with the apparent game-winner.

At that point, several thousand Giants' fans merrily skipped out of the park and told their family, friends and favorite barkeeper all about the great victory. Imagine their reactions the next morning when they picked up the newspaper.

Unaware of the Gill play, Merkle replicated baseball custom and peeled off about 30 feet before second base toward the Giants' clubhouse beyond center field. His strides got jauntier when an ecstatic Mathewson joined him.

THE WORM TURNS

Center-fielder Hofman fielded the ball and tossed it wide of a panting Evers at second base. Ever the jokester, Circus Solly decided to throw a curveball, according to his sportswriter friend, Hugh Keough.

The cantankerous "Iron Man" McGinnity was coaching third base in place of Luther "Dummy" Taylor, a starting pitcher who couldn't hear or talk but loved to have fun. A few weeks earlier, Taylor objected to O'Day's decision to continue a rainy game by wearing rubber boots and holding a canary-yellow umbrella in the coach's box. O'Day, who knew sign language, silently communicated a ban from the box, an ejection and a $25 fine.

The Iron Man—sensing those conniving Cubs were up to no good—barged into the fray, wrested the ball away from one of the Bruins and heaved it into the stands.

Cubs' reserve pitcher Kroh sprang from his customary spot on the bench, clocked the Giants' fan who had the ball and delivered it to Evers. More likely, Kroh found and handed over a different ball.

Flashing his creepiest bony-faced sneer, Evers stood on second base, held aloft the elusive baseball as if he had just recovered the Hope diamond and screamed for the force-out call...again.

Tinker demanded the call from Emslie while Chance stalked O'Day, fate's mandatory choice as this game's home-plate umpire.

Emslie had gotten up and looked to first base to confirm that Bridwell touched that bag. He swore he missed the entire swirl of activity at second base right in front of him and that he did not see whether Merkle touched second but did notice the youngster strolling toward the clubhouse.

O'Day, anticipating exactly what the Cubs would do so soon after their shared Gill experience, observed all the goings-on at second base.

Most of the 20,000 Giants' fans remained and invaded the field. The procedure when a game ended was for the ushers to open the gates and let the fans onto the field. The reality, however, was that the fans didn't wait for permission. They hopped over short walls and ducked under ropes the very second a game was over.

The postgame photos of September 23 resemble an ant convention. But the pictures could not convey the confusion and anger those Giants' fans must have felt. Triumphant after McCormick's apparent score, they soon wondered what all the discussion was about. Word wafted about that Chicago was appealing something or other.

Uncertainty quickly turned into hostility. Chance repelled angry Giants' fans while pursuing O'Day.

CLEAR AS MUD

At some point, O'Day said Merkle did not touch second base and called the force-out, negating the run and making it a 1–1 tie game. One can understand that the umpire, out of self-preservation, did not grab a megaphone, stand on a soapbox and yell out the bad news to thousands of froth-mouthed New York fans. Each fighting off throngs, Emslie and O'Day barely reached the small equipment shack that doubled as the umpires' dressing room.

A few seconds earlier, Mathewson suddenly heard Evers' crazed crowing back in the infield and urged Merkle to go back and touch second base. Too late.

Pulliam witnessed the game and the ensuing turmoil. He stayed away from the fray and then asked his umpires to submit written reports. They both related the following: Base umpire Emslie didn't see the play. Emslie asked O'Day—home-plate umpire and crew chief—if he did. O'Day said he did and that the Cubs touched second in possession of the ball before Merkle got there. Emslie, receiving this information from his partner, made the force-out call on the field. O'Day said the force-out meant that the run did not count, hence a 1–1 tie game.

It was pretty obvious the two arbiters huddled and hatched matching stories—heavy on what they felt was proper protocol—to protect their behinds. No one saw or heard Emslie make the out call. Many observers said that O'Day did. Bottom line: the umpiring crew made a call.

In his report, O'Day added two points—that he did not ask to have the field cleared because it was too dark to continue play, and that McGinnity committed interference.

In a rare interview six years later, O'Day told *The Sporting Life* that he made the out call, and it was because of the interference, not the Rule 59 issue. This was typical of the entire Merkle saga and aftermath. One central character after another added confusion instead of clarity.

Pulliam read the reports and, at 10 p.m., announced to the press that he was backing his umpires' call: 1–1 tie game. His decision infuriated everyone.

Brush, as irate as a baseball owner ever has been, screamed that he would not allow a game "honestly won" to be "jobbed off like diamonds on the installment plan." McGraw was livid. Mathewson promised that he would quit baseball forever if the victory was taken away and it cost his team the pennant. No one held him to it.

The bombastic Murphy demanded a forfeit—to go into the books as a 9–0 Cubs' victory—because O'Day made the proper rulebook call, it wasn't that dark and the home team was responsible for clearing the field to resume play.

"We can't supply brains to the New York club's dumb players," said Murphy, inflaming the situation while dumping on Merkle.

The writers felt the adrenaline rush of a big, juicy, sensational story. Baseball was about to hit the front pages. It was vital to hit a home run with the leads of their stories. Their editors would add the splashy headlines. Low as they were, standards of journalism regarding objectivity and factual accuracy were about to take a pounding. The writers' accounts wildly contradicted one another on the details and, with few exceptions, showed blatant New York-or-Chicago bias.

DESIGNATED GOAT

With deadlines beckoning, the press got busy burying young Merkle:

"A one-legged man with a noodle is better than a bonehead."

—Gym Bagley, *New York Evening Mail,* September 25

"Censurable stupidity on the part of player Merkle in yesterday's game....placed the New York team's chances of winning the pennant in jeopardy."

—*New York Times,* September 24.

"If only [Merkle] would run to second base when it is required—which reminds us of a man who had a thousand-dollar back and a ten-cent head. In fact, all our boys did rather well if Fred Merkle could gather the idea into his noodle that baseball custom does not permit a runner to take a shower and some light lunch in the clubhouse on the way to second."

—*New York Herald,* September 24

"Minor-league brains lost the Giants a game after they had it cleanly and fairly won."

—Charles Dryden, *Chicago Tribune,* September 24, referring to the "fat-headed Merkle."

"No plays came up in which Merkle had to think, so he got by."

—Jack Ryder, *Cincinnati Enquirer,* September 26, after the kid saw brief action the previous day

Accompanying the articles, several cartoons depicted Merkle with an outsized forehead, the standard visual exaggeration for stupidity. One showed him fleeing in his Giants' uniform to the "Coast of Labrador." Along with the "Bonehead" tag, the press called him "Leather Skull" and "Ivory Pate." Fans added the four-letter words that the sportswriters could not.

Merkle was crestfallen even before the newspapers came out. He couldn't eat dinner and stayed in his room the whole night. Over the next two weeks, he lost clumps of hair and at least 10 pounds of body weight. Not wanting to burden the team, he offered to quit. McGraw staunchly supported Merkle, and so did everyone in the Giants' organization.

HOW TO TICK OFF EVERYONE

September 24 marked the end of the four-game Giants-Cubs series and the last scheduled meeting between the two teams. One or both were booked with other games every day through October 7.

Pulliam had a brief window to nip this thing in the bud. Replay the game the next day as part of a double-header due to the constraints of the remaining schedule, and move on.

He instead announced a tedious process in which one team had five days to protest, the other team had five days to counter and the league's board of directors had five days to consider the evidence and announce its final decision.

The Cubs weren't waiting around for the deliberate Pulliam. The single game on the 24th was scheduled for 3 p.m. Doubleheaders started at 1:30 p.m. At 1:30 p.m., the visitors took the field in full uniform to play off the tie game. Kroh, the last Chicago pitcher who would be starting against the Giants, threw five warm-up pitches from the mound with a straight face. The umps and McGraw's team were nowhere in sight, leaving only the early-arriving New York fans to hiss at the hated Cubs and their theatrics.

Let's play two! Chicago, insisting it was ready to play and its opponent wasn't, demanded a second victory by forfeit in as many days. No dice, of course, but another bargaining chip to hurl at poor Pulliam.

When O'Day showed up for the afternoon contest, the Giants and their fans barely could restrain themselves. "Hey, Hank, why don't you wear a 'C' on your shirt?" yelled a red-faced Bresnahan.

The Gothams calmed down enough to win 5–4. Donlin doubled, tripled and knocked in four runs. The Cubs fought back from a 5–zip deficit with three runs off Wiltse in the top of the seventh. Entering with none out, Mathewson gave up a run-scoring single, then blanked Chicago for the duration.

The Pirates and Willis downed host Brooklyn 6–1 to complete a three-game sweep. New York (88–50) was now only a game ahead of Chicago and Pittsburgh, each at 90–54.

The first death from the Merkle controversy occurred back in Chicago. A heated argument developed between Giants' fan George Brooks and Cubs' fan Thomas Crocker. Settling the dispute with a bat, Brooks fractured Crocker's skull, killing him.

This was baseball, not war, but that chalk line was disappearing fast.

FATE CLOSES IN

FANS WATCH DETROIT FREE PRESS SCOREBOARD DURING
AL PENNANT DECIDING GAME

The Giants, leading by one game and three in the loss column, still controlled the pennant outcome. Besides the unresolved Merkle game, the New Yorkers would finish with 15 contests against noncontenders, including their next 8 at home to complete a string of 22 straight at the Polo Grounds. After a train ride to Philly for four games, they'd come right back home for the last three against lowly Boston.

Favorable position or not, New York stood on shaky ground. Doyle was on crutches, and Bresnahan, Donlin and Seymour were playing hurt. McGraw, facing 10 games and 4 doubleheaders over the next week, already had overworked Mathewson and Wiltse.

Fifth-place Cincinnati quickly darkened the Giants' outlook, defeating Marquard and McGinnity to sweep a twinbill 7–1 and 5–2 on September 25.

In his belated, ballyhooed debut, an admittedly nervous Marquard allowed a respectable two earned runs in five innings. The New York press, unhesitant to torch another young Giant, thought it reasonable to rename the kid "The $11,000 Lemon" instead of "The $11,000 Peach" after his first and only appearance of the season. Marquard would go on to earn 201 victories and immortality in Cooperstown. On the other end of the age spectrum, McGinnity was ineffective in the last start of his Hall of Fame career.

COVELESKI, THE SECOND "GIANT KILLER"

After winning four in a row, the Giants licked their chops before the second game of a doubleheader September 29. Warming up for fourth-place Philadelphia was 22-year-old lefty Harry Coveleski, who recently had returned from the minors. New York sent him there way back on April 17, routing the youngster in the third inning of a 14–2 laugher. For the season, the rookie would appear in only five games—four against the Giants.

Coveleski blanked the Giants 7–0, easily besting rookie counterpart Doc Crandall.

New York ended its turned-sour homestand with a 2–1 win the next day. The Giants and Phils headed to Philadelphia for a second straight four-game series.

A game but tired Matty barely hung on for a 4–3 win in the first of a pair October 1. On one day of rest, Coveleski defeated New York and Wiltse 6–2 in the second game. That one hurt. McGraw needed every victory, but especially when using either of his two best pitchers.

The Giants breezed 7–2 the next day to set up a Coveleski–Mathewson matchup October 3. It was the third start in five days for both pitchers and Matty's sixth appearance in 11 days.

The kid came out on top 3–2, giving grateful Chicago and Pittsburgh openings. Matty's error allowed the deciding run in the sixth inning. Coveleski climaxed his historic trifecta by mowing down Donlin, Seymour and Devlin to strand runners on second and third with no one out in the ninth.

The sportswriters, most of them misspelling his name throughout the week, anointed Coveleski as the second "Giant Killer" of the season. Preferring two ethnic slurs to one, the *New York Herald* observed, "[Coveleski] seems to have the Indian sign on the stickers, big and little from Coogan's Bluff. He hails from Shamokin, Pennsylvania, in the coal field, and is a Polak."

"Big Ed" Reulbach

Coveleski struggled the next two years—the vengeful Giants playing constant head games with him—before posting three straight 20-win seasons in the AL with the Tigers. Younger brother Stanley Coveleski was a righty pitcher and Hall of Famer.

Hitting on all cylinders, Pittsburgh quietly went on a 13–1 run—winning its last two in New York and then going 3–0 at Brooklyn and 2–1 at Boston before sweeping the Cardinals 3–0, 3–0 in Pittsburgh and St. Louis.

In the same must-win boat, Chicago rode a 22–4 surge. The Cubs completed a 19-day, five-city road trip by winning seven of their next eight outings—going 3–0 at Brooklyn and 4–1 at Cincinnati. Down to their last strike at the raucous Palace, the Reds got a game-winning, bases-loaded single from Lobert—now a hero—for the Bruins' only setback of the week.

Saving a worn-out pitching staff, the Cubs' "Big Ed" Reulbach started both ends of a doubleheader in Brooklyn on September 26 and hurled complete-game shutouts, the only pitcher ever to accomplish the feat. He allowed but eight hits in 5–0 and 3–0 victories during his personal streak of 44 consecutive scoreless innings.

Reulbach, who had a weak left eye but a wicked curveball, improved from overly to effectively wild down the stretch, going 7–0 to finish at 24–7 in a yeoman 297.2 innings. He led the NL in winning percentage for the third straight season. An underrated star of the Cubs' dynasty, he went 94–32 from 1906 through 1910. Reulbach compiled winning streaks of 17 and 14 games to become the only pitcher in the modern era with two stretches of 14 consecutive victories or more.

WINDY CITY SHOWDOWNS

The anticipation of the two enormous games to be played simultaneously in Chicago on Sunday afternoon, October 4 was simply off the charts.

On the AL side, the White Sox (86–63) faced elimination by the defending league-champion Tigers (89–61) in the first of a three-game set. The Cleveland Naps (88–63), nicknamed by a vote of their fans for Hall of Fame player-manager Napoleon "Nap" Lajoie, remained alive.

The St. Louis Browns—alternately helped and hurt by left-handed pitcher Rube Waddell, the flakiest baseball player of all time—recently had fallen out of the race. The New York Highlanders, the early-season leader, had imploded amid accusations that Hal Chase was throwing games.

The AL race had taken center stage two days earlier when Cleveland's Addie Joss, needing only 74 pitches, threw a perfect game for a 1–0 victory over Chicago in a legendary duel of Hall of Fame pitchers. "Big Ed" Walsh, a spitballer, struck out 15 Naps and allowed only four hits. The game's only run scored on Walsh's wild pitch.

Joss won 24 games, hurled nine shutouts and posted a 1.16 earned run average. In his 11 losses, the Naps scored 11 runs. He no-hit the White Sox again in 1910, becoming the only pitcher to turn the trick twice against one team. Joss's brilliant career was cut short after nine seasons; he was diagnosed with tubercular meningitis and died at age 31.

Walsh (40–15, 1.42, 464 innings) notched a season for the ages. He stands as the last pitcher to win 40 games and the last to throw 400 innings. He nearly matched Reulbach's doubleheader shutout feat by winning a pair and allowing only one run September 29.

That followed a shameful incident on September 28 after a game ending in darkness and a 10-inning tie. According to several sources, a prominent Chicago attorney and White Sox club rooter named Robert Cantwell knocked out umpire John Kerin with one punch, breaking Kerin's nose and ending his season. Cantwell paid a court fine and bragged that the publicity helped his law practice.

The Cubs (97–55) had to win the make-up game against Pittsburgh to stay alive. The Pirates (98–55) would be down to the remote mathematical chance of a three-way tie if they lost. The Giants (95–55) were goners if the Bucs won and therefore had to root for the hated Cubs, which everyone else found hilarious. A few other scenarios depended on the league's decision of the Merkle game as well as a possible rainout of any of the three Giants' games against Boston.

A crowd estimated at 5,000—including Giants' and Doves' players—convened at the Polo Grounds to watch the electronic-scoreboard version of the showdown in Chicago. Workers transported the board from Madison Square Garden, which had featured several recent games.

Traffic bottlenecked in Manhattan as fans watched the storefront boards and spilled into the streets. New York's phone company ordered its operators to relay the score of the game to callers in an effort to unclog the lines. "Mrs. McGillicutty, sorry about your husband's heart attack. I'll connect you with the hospital in a moment, but I know you'll want to know about the ballgame. That little jerk Evers just...."

An estimated 50,000 Pirates' fans headed to a rally in downtown Pittsburgh. Men stationed atop newspaper buildings bellowed game updates through megaphones. Inside, the editors began preparing their first-ever Sunday evening editions.

Chicago's Orchestra Hall set up two boards on opposite ends of the room to treat swivel-headed fans to a doubleheader of sorts. Going to an extreme to prevent a mud-field postponement and big-revenue loss, Murphy borrowed the world's only infield tarpaulin, shipping in the enormous canvas from Pittsburgh.

The Cubs attracted 30,000 to West Side Grounds while—just 3.6 miles away—the Sox drew 26,000 to South Side Park. Both crowds set several attendance records and were way over capacity. In something less than a peaceful Sabbath, mobs of White Sox fans destroyed fences to gain entrance.

The White Sox stayed alive by beating the Tigers 3–1. The "other" three-team race would continue at least to Monday, the next to last day of the AL's regular season.

The Hitless Wonders scored all three of their runs without any base hits. The winning pitcher was stout right-hander Frank Smith, nicknamed "Piano Mover" for his strength and "Nig" for his dark complexion. (He was at least the fifth player of such skin hue to be called Nig.) Smith, who didn't get along with player-manager Fielder Jones, left the team for seven weeks during the summer. Upon his return, he pitched as magnificently as Walsh, but Jones still seethed with resentment.

Irony accompanied the tension of the Cubs–Pirates tilt. Aces Brown and Willis had matched up in the Gill game with O'Day behind the plate; their roles were the same exactly one month later. Bookies favored neither side. The steely Cubs rarely lost a game they had to win, but the Pirates were 56–20 in road games and 12–9 against Chicago.

The Cubs prevailed 5–2, thanks in part to two uncharacteristic Wagner errors. Brown, who was a good-hitting pitcher, and Evers each scored a run and knocked in another.

Naturally, there was controversy. Pittsburgh's Ed Abbaticchio smashed a liner down the right-field line and into the crowd in the ninth inning with Wagner on first and no one out. O'Day called the ball foul, and the Pirates flipped out. O'Day consulted with his base umpire, who supported the call. The woman who was struck by the ball threatened to sue for damages while insisting the ball was fair. Another woman gave birth in the stands during the game; she had no opinion about the play. With the extra-base hit nullified, Brown quietly retired the side.

Refusing to whine, Dreyfuss and Clarke congratulated the Cubs in their clubhouse and told the press the better team had won. The classy Pirates were essentially gone but not forgotten. Before their finale, the Bucs erased a five-game deficit with their 13–1 charge. Led by the congenial Wagner in his greatest season, Pittsburgh went a scorching 83–41 after digging that early 15–15 hole.

To Err Is Human; to "Merkle" Is Hilarious

New Yorkers, granted an unintended reprieve by Chicago, collectively exhaled and returned to their new hobby of stomping on Merkle.

"I call my cane Merkle because it has a bonehead on it," cracked a Vaudeville comedian appearing on Broadway. The New York newspapers lauded the new act, and the public lapped it up.

"Merkle" suddenly became a popular verb, meaning to fail to show up, arrive tardy or mess up in any way. Sometimes it was a noun, replacing either boner or bonehead.

"You Merkled. Late for work fourth time this month, you Merkle. One more Merkle, and you're gone."

Looking wan, Merkle kept his head down, sat at the end of the bench and rarely played. He actually didn't hear too many bonehead taunts from the crowd over the last two weeks. Giants' fans whispered and pretended to look past him. The proverbial elephant in the room had shifted to the baseball diamond.

It's difficult for a baseball team to sweep any opponent three games straight, which was New York's challenge. Some believed Boston would lie down because so many personal ties linked the two organizations. McGann, still angry, and the other Doves belied such talk by playing all out. The other subplot involved McGraw's delicate pitching decisions. Preferring to rest his arm-weary ace for the possible one-game pennant battle with Chicago, he took a calculated but huge risk by not using Mathewson in any of the three games.

McGraw's strategy paid off as the Giants handily took all three. Ames, who had been beating inferior teams consistently, won the first and third games. Wiltse dodged enough bullets in the Tuesday contest.

AL: Down to the Wire

Meanwhile, the White Sox, behind Walsh, made it two in a row over the Tigers on Monday to draw within a half-game of Detroit. Cleveland lost the first game of a doubleheader to St. Louis and was eliminated. The Naps were furious that they had to play a pair. They hotly disputed a call the day before that resulted in—what else?—a tie game and a replay instead of a victory.

The AL race came down to a one-game, take-all affair on Tuesday the 6th. The victor—Tigers or White Sox—would win the pennant.

Jones couldn't bring himself to give the ball to the red-hot but formerly AWOL Piano Mover Smith. He started a dead-tired Doc White on one day of rest. Owner Charles Comiskey fired Jones for the decision, which may not have broken Jones' heart. The outstanding Sox skipper had tired of holding together a team filled with unhappy players underpaid by the penny-pinching Comiskey.

Before another record crowd of 27,000 that included several resting Cubs, the Tigers dominated 7–0 to win their second straight pennant. Cobb, still as popular with his mates as the plague but finally in a post-matrimonial groove, lashed a two-run triple to key a four-run rally. A big deficit was insurmountable for the punchless Sox, who hadn't homered in 10 weeks. Walsh, out of gas, relieved the pummeled White in a lost cause.

Detroit (90–63, .588), Cleveland (90–64, .584), Chicago (88–64, .579). The final AL standings exposed Ban Johnson and company's terrible decision to go by winning percentages instead of mandating the completion of all games with a bearing on the pennant outcome. Among the three contenders, only the Naps played a full 154-game schedule.

To the chagrin of the Naps and White Sox, the Tigers never had to play a make-up game with Washington, which might have started 20-year-old right-hander Walter Johnson, a fireballing sidearmer. Having hurled three shutouts over a four-day span in September, the "Big Train" was already on his way to becoming one of the greatest pitchers of all time.

Chicago didn't get to make up two rainouts—one against the faded Browns, the other against a bad Philadelphia A's team. The Tigers, a far better team than Washington, probably would have been a slight favorite against the Big Train. Their 91st victory would have closed out the Naps and White Sox. But Detroit—and Chicago—should have been required to play 154 games. The prospects of either a dramatic two- or three-way playoff were consigned forever to the what-if bin.

The American League and National League races of 1908 had two factors in common. They featured fantastic, riveting baseball and qualified as two of the greatest pennant battles of all time. They also were marred by league mismanagement. As tremendous as these races were, they might have been even better.

One of them was over, and the other was about to spin completely out of control.

GAME THAT HAD NO EQUAL
POLO GROUNDS CROWD WATCHING AND FANS LEAVING AFTER LOSS

The Madhouse Pennant Tiebreaker

BRUSH COULD NOT CONTROL CROWD OR OUTCOME

ortoises sped by Pulliam as the days passed without a final ruling. It had been nearly two weeks since the Merkle game. Sportswriters accused the president of dragging his feet deliberately in hopes that a team would pull away and render a decision moot. The anxiety level of New Yorkers was especially high. Down deep, they anticipated—and dreaded—a tie-game verdict, but they wanted to know one way or the other.

Picking up where we left off, the burdensome process went like so: Brush formally protested. Murphy appealed for a second instead of first forfeit. The Cubs waived their five days to reply to the Giants' protest, which should have sped things up, but didn't. Enlisting two attorneys, Brush decorated Pulliam's desk with affidavits—eyewitness accounts from purely objective Giants' fans swearing that Merkle touched the base first. Pulliam recommended a tie-game ruling, and the matter passed to the board of directors. Brush elicited a creative version from Merkle himself and threw that on top of the pile.

Pulliam took away his, Murphy's and Dreyfuss's votes and left the decision to the other three board members—owners Garry Herrmann of Cincinnati, George Dovey of Boston and Charles Ebbets of Brooklyn. Before they even sat down, each was accused of bias toward New York or Chicago based on past relationships and business interests.

One of the New York papers reported that Herrmann believed Rule 59 shouldn't apply on an obvious game-winning hit to the outfield; Dovey felt the same but favored a do-over; Ebbets—completely wimping out—thought the league president should be backed no matter what. In other words, two of them implicitly sided with Merkle, and the third took no position whatsoever regarding whether to go by rule or tradition.

Needing a unanimous vote, they "compromised" in private and agreed on the inevitable.

Thirteen days after the Merkle game—midday, Tuesday, October 6—Pulliam announced the board's decision: 1–1 tie game; weather permitting, replay the contest in its entirety at 3 p.m. Thursday, October 8, at the Polo Grounds.

The president's press release went way beyond an official explanation of the play, the umpires' decision, the disallowing of both protests, his recommendation and the committee's final ruling:

> *The decision of the directors (in part) is as follows: There can be no question but that the game should have been won by New York had it not been for the reckless, careless, inexcusable blunder of one player, Merkle....Merkle should have had only one thing on his mind, to reach second base in safety....We can therefore come to no other conclusion that the New York club lost a well-earned victory as the result of a stupid play of one of its members.*

Pulliam jumped on the bandwagon and fried Merkle. The only thing missing from the president's document was a Merkle bonehead cartoon. But why? Pulliam was an insecure but not mean-spirited man. The intense criticism he received during the Merkle affair pushed him over the edge. Desperate to salvage his image, he went overboard in faulting the young player.

How late was the decision? McGraw, heading into the middle game of the Boston series, had been forced to make crucial pitching decisions without knowing if there would be a replayed game against the Cubs. The Chicago players, collecting rust, watched the other league's one-game pennant showdown while wondering if they'd play one any time soon. The Pirates, still mathematically alive for a three-way playoff, had split for their respective homes all over the country two days prior. Most fans were unaware of the decision until they saw Wednesday morning's newspapers, giving them only a day to make plans for the pennant-deciding game.

Not unexpectedly, many New York players and fans—plus several writers—wanted the Giants to boycott the game in the firm conviction they already had won it fair and square. They would play. But they and their supporters would enter the arena with chips on their shoulders the size of boulders.

Right on cue, loud-mouthed Murphy ratcheted up the antipathy and threw in another swipe at Merkle. "We will play them Thursday and we'll lick 'em too. We'll make it so decisive that no bone-headed baserunning can cast a shadow of doubt on the contest," he boasted.

Hyping it from a ballgame to mortal combat, the New York press stirred Giants' fans into a higher state of frenzy. "That the game will be a struggle to the death is certain. The town is in the grip of the greatest excitement, fringed with nervous prostration. It is rumored that several sanitariums are constructing additions to take care of baseball 'bugs' resulting from the last few weeks of the campaign," shrieked the *Herald.*

The newspapers drove up the betting action while putting more pressure on the home team.

"Several large personal wagers were laid last night at even money. In all probability, the Giants will be a 10 to 9 favorite. Everyone in this city has unlimited faith in Mc-Graw, in Mathewson and in each and every individual on the Giant roster."

—W. J. MacBeth, *New York American*

Because of the league's tardy ruling, the Cubs had to scramble just to get to New York by the morning of the game. Murphy reserved a car for his team on the luxurious Twentieth Century Limited supertrain, paying $600 for the 18-hour trip—$200 more but 10 hours faster than for a regular train. Kling, attending to business in another state, barely made it to Chicago for the Wednesday afternoon departure.

Just the Usual Pregame: Riot, Bribes, Death Threats

Pulliam selected Klem and Johnstone to officiate the biggest game in the history of baseball. This was a plum assignment for both arbiters but especially the ambitious Klem, who was only in his fourth season.

UMPIRE BILL KLEM CALLED A CLEAN GAME

On the eve of the game, Dr. Joseph Creamer—the Giants' full-time physician—offered Klem $2,500 to throw the game to New York. Johnstone, a veteran umpire, was approached by gamblers with similar offers and claimed to have witnessed the attempted bribe of Klem. The umps reported the incident the next morning to NL Secretary John Heydler. Pulliam was in Detroit preparing for the World Series. It was too late to change the umpiring assignments, which could explain why both arbiters kept quiet overnight.

As Klem walked down a dark runway leading to the field before the game, Creamer emerged from the shadows again, waved the money in front of the umpire and reiterated that Klem would be set for life if he delivered a Giants' victory. "Now take that, will you, Bill," pleaded Creamer. Klem and Johnstone rebuffed the offers and called a clean game, but the stench of the incidents lingered.

In its first and only successful attempt at crowd control, Giants' management deployed watchmen around the Polo Grounds through the night to prevent kids from sneaking in and hiding under seats.

Mathewson awoke in the morning and confided to his wife that his arm felt dead despite having not pitched since Saturday. The Cubs reached Grand Central Station at 9:30 a.m. and were welcomed by thousands of foul-mouthed Giants' fans.

That was mild compared to the death threats the Cubs had already received—six directed to Brown and one each to Evers and Evers' mother.

The box office opened at 11 a.m. Brush did not allow advance sales in an attempt to keep tickets away from scalpers. The game was sold out by noon. Forty-five minutes later, Giants' management closed the gates. That decision touched off a riot.

Although there were no advanced sales, many fans held season tickets or passes to all games. They could not get in if they arrived past 12:45—still more than two hours before the scheduled start time. The thousands of fans who made the trip from other states intended to get in one way or another. So did the fiercest of local Giants' rooters. Wall Street looked like a ghost town as nearly every banker and broker headed to the park.

Forming a football-style "flying wedge," human bodies repeatedly battered a wooden fence beyond the outfield until it splintered. That let in thousands of fans. Another contingent attempted to burn down a fence. Less successful, they were hosed down by firemen. Still another gaggle of rascals set up a long plank from the subway platform to a Polo Grounds fence, creating a sliding chute right into the park. Most failed, funneling to waiting authorities.

At least 10,000 ticketless fans found their way inside. Brush had increased capacity to the 28,000-to-30,000 range, but the crowd approached 40,000. The grandstands were so packed that 34-year-old Ed Wheeler was squeezed off the top row, plunged to the ground and broke his leg.

Albert Spalding, now 58, made the trip all the way from California. He pulled up in his chauffeur-driven car holding four box seats and a season's pass and was told he couldn't get in. Spalding never accepted "no" from anyone his entire life. A gate was raised to let in an ambulance—neither the first nor last summoned that day—and the irascible one grabbed on.

Brush, ticked at several sportswriters for their coverage of the Merkle issue, sprang a surprise by giving some of the seats on press row to celebrities. Hughie Fullerton, the colorful sportswriter of the *Chicago Examiner,* showed up and found actor Louis Mann in his seat. Mann wouldn't budge, and the usher responded with a shrug. Fullerton shrugged back and sat on Mann's lap through the entire game, writing a 5,000-word account. The incident helped to spur the formation of the first baseball writers' association only a month later, which certainly wasn't Brush's intent.

Even among the blue-blooded, propriety gave way to urgency. Henry Taft and George Wickersham got in by slithering along sewer pipes. Taft was the brother of the country's next president, Wickersham soon to be our attorney general.

Fans Gone Wild

Counting the nearly 40,000 on the inside, an estimated 250,000 people descended on the scene. A few weeks earlier, the police commissioner changed his policy and began to place officers within the Polo Grounds as well as on the outside. He assigned about 300 coppers for the big game, which proved helpful but woefully inadequate.

Sleazebags kept selling counterfeit tickets, causing rashes of fights to break out after the buyers realized they had been duped. Pickpockets had a filching field day among the masses.

From the press box the skyline everywhere was human heads. They were located on grandstands, roofs, fences, "L" structures, electric light poles and in the distance smokestacks, chimneys, advertising signs and copings of apartment houses.

—*New York Evening Telegram*

The subway trains barely could run. People were on top of the cars, all over the platforms and scaffoldings and dangerously near the tracks. An off-duty fireman named Henry McBride perched himself precariously on a pillar above the tracks, lost his grip and fell to his death. Policemen repelled others who instantly wanted to try out McBride's spot.

The exterior vantage points, including a crammed Coogan's Bluff, afforded a partial view of the field at best. "Never in the history of the game have there been so many to see a game who didn't see it," famously observed the *New York Times'* W. J. Lampton.

The Cubs entered the fray expecting the worst. The crowd managed to exceed their expectations. "I never heard anybody or any set of men called as many foul names as the Giants fans called us that day from the time we showed up till it was over," recalled Brown.

Perhaps noticing the full-blown riot all around them, officials decided to start the game at 2:45 instead of 3 o'clock. Shortened or not, the time used for batting practice was supposed to be divided evenly between the two teams. McGraw let his Giants consume 15 minutes and stopped the Cubs after 5.

He dispatched McGinnity—essentially bench fodder today—to home plate to pick a fight with Chance in the hope that Chicago's Peerless Leader would take the bait and get ejected or injured. Either would do nicely. Iron Man got in Chance's face, cursed him a blue streak, stepped on his feet with his spikes and spit right in his face.

Chance calmly walked away and instructed every Cub to pick out a Giants' player and "call 'em everything in the book." They eagerly obliged.

Ten minutes before the game, Giants' fans erupted in cheers as their hero—looking more regal than ever in a full-length white linen duster—strode in from the outfield in one of the most stirring introductions in the annals of sports.

Even the Cubs were impressed. "I can still see Christy Mathewson making his lordly entrance," reflected Brown years later.

The audience was unaware that Matty, even after warming up, had just whispered to Bresnahan the same thing he had told his wife. That wasn't New York's only problem. Five Giants' starters played hurt. The gimpy Doyle was reduced to pinch-hitting, and McGraw intended to keep Merkle on the bench rather than throw him to the wolves.

WE NOW INTERRUPT THIS RIOT
FOR A BALLGAME

Lieb, who covered baseball for nearly seven decades, called it the greatest game ever played. "For sheer dramatics, for pathos, tragedy, hatred, heroics, intrigue and chicanery, and for its later recriminations and reverberations, this game never has had an equal," he said.

Pfiester the Giant Killer took the hill in the bottom of the first inning, hoping that Bonesetter Reese's manual cures for torn tendons had some staying power. It didn't look like it.

The southpaw plunked Tenney and walked Herzog. Pfiester struck out Bresnahan, and catcher Kling pretended to drop and lose sight of the ball. Herzog, falling for the trick, stretched his lead. Kling gunned him out for a costly double play. Donlin swatted a double to score Tenney, and Seymour walked.

Chance didn't hesitate and beckoned his three-fingered ace from the outfield bullpen. Brown maneuvered quickly through pawing Giants' fans, privately worrying that this would be the time for a lunatic to act on a death threat.

He had worked in 11 of the past 14 games, which was the main reason he didn't get the start. The strain didn't show. Brown struck out Devlin to end the inning, the Giants silently ruing not scoring more than one run.

No one could have been rooting harder for the Giants than Merkle, who still had a chance to escape infamy if his team won. Mathewson remembered the rookie's reaction when the Giants took the early lead: "For the first time in a month, Merkle smiled. He was drawn up in the corner of the bench, pulling away from the rest of us as if he had some contagious disease or was quarantined."

The crowd whooped it up in the second inning when Matty picked off Chance, who had singled. Circus Solly was ejected for arguing the call too vehemently. Del Howard replaced him.

Matty's numbed arm caught up with him in the third inning. Tinker, his tormentor, was set to lead off. The pitcher motioned Seymour to play a deeper center field. Instead, Seymour played his own hunch—a short liner—and remained shallow. Tinker walloped a drive over his head, and Seymour compounded his initial mistake with two more. He started in and couldn't retreat in time. He made a play on the ball as it rolled into the crowd, resulting in a triple instead of a ground-rule double.

Kling singled in Tinker, Brown sacrificed Kling to second and Sheckard flew out. One more out, and the damage would be limited to the one tying run. Nope. Evers walked, and the long-slumping but recently hot

Wildfire Schulte belted an RBI double down the line. Chance, collecting the second of his three hits, smartly took an outside pitch to right field to knock in the Cubs' third and fourth runs.

With the score 4–1, many dejected New York fans were seen weeping, the cumulative emotions of nearly a six-month race and all of its drama suddenly overcoming them.

The Giants had one more rally in them. In the seventh, Donlin and McCormick led off with singles, and Bridwell walked to load the bases with none out. With McGraw passing on Merkle, the limping Doyle pinch-hit for Mathewson and floated a foul pop well behind home plate. Kling somehow focused on the ball and speared it near the fence as thrown bottles, mugs, derby hats and cushions flew by him. Tenney's sacrifice fly produced a run before Herzog grounded into the third out.

Fights in the stands caused delays toward the end, but the two outstanding teams still completed the game in a snappy hour and 40 minutes. Brown, who allowed but four hits on the day, retired New York on four pitches in the ninth. In his retirement years, he said it was his most satisfying win and that he never pitched better.

The 4–2 victory earned the Cubs their third-straight pennant and capped a scintillating closing streak of 41–10 that remains unmatched in baseball history. At last, the standings were final: Chicago (99–55), one game better than New York and Pittsburgh (both 98–56).

FRANK "HUSK" CHANCE—THOUGH BEANED BY BASEBALLS
AND HIT WITH BOTTLES, ALWAYS "THE PEERLESS LEADER"

UGLY END

Then it got nasty again as the Cubs tried in vain to make it safely to the visitors' clubhouse. A fan rushed Chance and belted him in the neck, causing some cartilage damage. Someone slashed Pfiester's pitching shoulder with a knife. Tinker, Sheckard and Howard all were struck by thrown objects.

Once the Cubs got inside the clubhouse, the mob broke the windows and tried to break down the doors. Police officers felt it was a good time to pull out their revolvers. Brown and several other Cubs came up with a clever exit plan. Eschewing police escorts, they waited a while, disguised themselves in street clothes and blended anonymously into the crowd.

The scene in Chicago was pure bliss. People danced in long lines down State Street, tossed hats, waved bear flags and rang bells. Special newspaper editions turned into confetti.

Some of the articles that came out of New York the next day tore into their team and fans for poor behavior and sportsmanship.

"The scene yesterday was really the most disgraceful ever pulled off around here. McGinnity started a row.... Once when Kling was a chasing a foul....Is that baseball? Does that do New York any good? Gee whiz! If we can't lose a pennant without dirty work, let's quit altogether."

—Tad Dorgan, *New York Evening Journal.*

Brush and McGraw never got over the loss. Brush had medals made for his team, inscribed to the "Real Champions, 1908." He distributed the entire $10,000 sum of receipts from the final game to his players. Whenever McGraw was asked how many league titles he earned, he answered, "I won ten pennants, and they stole an 11th from me in the league office."

McGraw may never have grasped his culpability in the scapegoating of Merkle. He should have known about the Gill game and instructed his players to go all the way to the next base. That said, McGraw not only defended

Merkle to the hilt but also hit the nail on the head in pointing out that a team's fortunes encompass the full season, not one game or one play.

"It's criminal to say that Merkle is stupid and to blame the loss of the pennant on him. In the first place, he is one of the smartest and best players on this club and in not touching second base, he merely did as he had seen veteran players do ever since he's been in the league," McGraw insisted. "In the second place, he didn't cost us the pennant. We lost a dozen games we should have won this year. Yes, two dozen. Any one of them could have saved the pennant for us."

New York's sloppy defeats against bad teams early in the season came back to haunt the team. The Giants' 11–6 record down the stretch certainly didn't qualify as a "choke," but they gave the Cubs a chance with the doubleheader loss to Cincinnati and the three defeats to Coveleski.

The filming of baseball began in 1908 with the World Series but, unfortunately, not with the historic games of September 23 and October 8.

The Series was anticlimactic. The Cubs—led by Overall, Brown and Schulte—won four of five games and breezed to their second straight championship over the Tigers.

After 101 years, the Chicago National League ball club has yet to win its third title in the modern era.

Decades later, people who believe in such things began to speak of the "Curse of Merkle."

Apparently, the great Cubs' team of 1908 won only because of one key ruling that went in their favor, and that consumed more than a century's worth of luck.

Thus, Merkle somehow became responsible not only for the Giants losing in 1908 but also for the Cubs never winning again after that year. Nifty trick.

Sweep Under Rug

The season for the ages exhausted its participants. "I honestly believe that the 1908 race took more out of me than three ordinary seasons," reflected Cleveland's Lajoie.

No one needed rest more than Pulliam, but he did not have that luxury. Murphy was found to have scalped his own tickets to the '08 Series, and the National Commission—headed by league presidents Pulliam and Johnson—censured him for it. Next on the docket was far more serious: Creamer's attempts to buy off the umpires and who might have been behind him.

Unbelievably, Pulliam chose Brush—the owner of the team whose employee did the deed—to head the investigating committee. *The Sporting News* simply called the appointment "unfortunate."

Pulliam, Ebbets and Herrmann composed the rest of the committee. The interests of the two owners were nearly as conflicted as Brush's. A public scandal involving the sport and their league's cornerstone franchise could kill the golden goose.

Brush opened the initial meeting in December by falsely stating that the doctor wasn't a full-time Giants' employee. Then he claimed he was unaware of the hire all along. He almost certainly would have signed off on an expenditure of $2,800 for a new position.

Instead of conducting a thorough investigation, Brush redirected the committee's focus. He brought in lawyers who dwelled on whether the alleged bribes constituted a crime according to New York statutes and concluded they did not.

When the committee met again in February, Herrmann said that he heard Creamer had represented three Giants. Someone tried to black out key words in the official minutes, but the names of McGraw, Mathewson and Bresnahan were visible. The press didn't report that information, and there was no indication the committee asked any of the three to respond.

The waters got a lot muddier a decade later when Phillies' catcher Red Dooin revealed that a "noted catcher of the New York Giants"—meaning Bresnahan—dropped $40,000 on his lap to induce him to throw the final Giants–Phillies series in 1908. Dooin turned down the offer, but his story was confirmed by eyewitnesses, including a sportswriter who owned a piece of the Phillies and several of Dooin's teammates.

The committee, which never released Creamer's name throughout the entire process, announced its decision in April 1909. It banned the anonymous perpetrator from baseball for life after blabbing on about its desire to prosecute but having insufficient evidence to do so.

A couple of weeks later, the *Chicago Tribune's* Harvey Woodruff revealed Creamer's identity, but the attention of the writer's peers was on the new baseball season. Creamer denied any involvement, threatened to sue and drifted into oblivion. To the relief of baseball's establishment, the story died.

Many baseball historians have pointed their fingers directly at McGraw. He found and hired Creamer with management's approval. He and Bresnahan were very close. Everyone knew of McGraw's past gambling indiscretions and relationships with prominent bookmakers. Powerful people furnished Creamer—and Bresnahan before that—with lots of money to dangle and promises of more. The prevailing attitude on the Giants during and after the Merkle mess was that anything they did to get back at the league and the Cubs was justified. In an interview years later, Klem unwittingly cast suspicion on both himself and McGraw by volunteering that the umpire and the Giants' manager were friends who often dined together—a fraternization no-no.

Put all that together, and you've got nothing. As always, McGraw skated.

TRAGIC AFTERMATH

The Creamer ugliness was but one of many shady incidents threatening the integrity of the sport before, during and after 1908. Baseball's hierarchy always acted the same way. It got scared, did little about it and hoped it would go away. Baseball got what it deserved in 1919.

Pulliam, already buckling during the Merkle controversy, completely wigged out that winter. He began drinking heavily, spending money wildly, cursing at co-workers and threatening strangers. He told friends he needed to get away. In February, he addressed the owners with a rambling, incoherent speech. Several observers felt that he should be placed in a mental facility but took no action. He took a leave of absence—Heydler assuming his duties—and returned to work in no better state of mind in late June.

Harry Clay Pulliam left work early on the afternoon of July 28, 1909, went directly to his apartment at the New York Athletic Club, shot himself in the right temple at 9:30 p.m. and died the next morning at age 40.

To honor Pulliam, all games in both leagues were postponed on August 2, the day of his funeral. The only team that sent no one was the New York Giants.

"I didn't think a bullet to the head could hurt him," remarked McGraw.

SEASONED GIANT TEAMMATES
FRED MERKLE, ART WILSON AND BUCK HERZOG

MERKLE'S CAREER: PROFILE IN COURAGE

AN OLDER MERKLE AS A CUB

Pictures say 1,000 words. In the case of Merkle, they tell the whole story. He looks carefree before September 23, 1908, and—with few exceptions—visibly burdened thereafter. The strain is etched in his face, and the eyes reveal a deep hurt.

It was totally defensible for the Giants to hold onto the still-promising youngster in whom they had invested. But it also would have been an act of mercy to trade the scorned young man after his 1908 travails. A small-market American League team would have been ideal. Get him away from the NL, the cheap shots from New York's press and fans and the sarcastic thanks-for-the-pennant barbs from Chicago's leather-lungs.

Merkle remained a Giant for 10 years, transferred only a borough away to Brooklyn and finally moved out of the Big Apple—to the Cubs, of course. After a stint in the minors, it was back to New York as a coach and emergency player with the Yankees.

Deflecting the abuse as well as anyone possibly could have, Merkle endured as a fine, dependable player over a solid 16-year career.

But he wasn't that in 1909. In fact, he was a mess. McGraw's plan was to let Merkle phase out 37-year-old Tenney and play most of the time. McGraw gave the kid a $500 raise and encouraged him, but Merkle showed up underweight and depressed in spring training and never pulled out of his funk. He hit a feeble .191 with no homers and only 20 RBI in 79 games and 236 at-bats.

"Listen to them hoot. You're making a mistake to keep me here. They don't want me," Merkle told his manager.

McGraw replied, "I wish I had more players like you. Don't pay any attention to those weathercocks. They'll be cheering you the next time you make a good play."

His manager's faith paid off. Two years removed from the fateful play at second base, Merkle hit a powerful .292 with four homers and 70 ribbies over 144 games in 1910.

Merkle pulled a variation of the hidden-ball trick on Evers in the fifth inning of the first game of a doubleheader September 22, 1910—two years less a day after the famous game. Neither contest was important because the Cubs had clinched the pennant more than a week earlier. Merkle faked a throw back to the pitcher and tagged out the napping Evers a few feet off first base, completely reversing the roles of the bonehead and eagle-eyed veteran. But the sportswriters weren't about to change the roles they had previously assigned to the two players. They devoted somewhere between a paragraph and nothing to the play.

McGraw's rebuilding job was ready to bear fruit. Merkle and the rest of New York's baby bench brigade from '08 entered the early primes of their careers and helped the Giants win three straight NL pennants.

In 1911, Merkle hit .283, belted 12 homers—including a tape-measure shot in Cincinnati—knocked in 84 runs and stole 49 bases. He finished seventh in the NL MVP Chalmers Award voting.

He was a top-shelf performer again the following year despite missing 25 games with injuries. Merkle hit a career-high .309 with 11 homers, 84 RBI and 37 steals—placing 18th in Chalmers balloting.

In Case You Forgot His Nickname...

Merkle's clutch RBI single in the top of the 10th inning gave New York the lead over Boston in the final game of the 1912 World Series. This was neither the first nor last time he put himself in a position to be the hero.

Alas, Fred Snodgrass dropped a routine fly ball to center field to lead off the bottom of the frame. After a flyout and a walk, future Hall of Famer Tris Speaker lifted a foul fly not far from the first-base coaches' box. Catcher Chief Meyers hustled toward the ball. Matty converged and yelled for Meyers to make the play. Merkle was conflicted. He was closest but also aware that the pitcher is the traffic director on such plays. He backed off. The ball fell to the ground.

Given new life, Speaker singled to spark Boston's winning rally. The New York papers slammed Snodgrass for his "$30,000 Muff"—the difference between the winning and losing team's shares. Little was said about Snodgrass's tremendous catch of a Harry Hooper line drive earlier in the game.

Merkle hardly went unscathed. Not surprisingly, the press ran a volley of "Bonehead Merkle Does It Again" headlines. The one fallen popup dwarfed his outstanding regular-season performance and otherwise fine work in the Series.

McGraw defended Snodgrass and—for the first time—hung Merkle out to dry. "Snodgrass didn't lose the game. It was lost when Merkle didn't catch Speaker's foul.

We were all yelling at him from the bench that it was his ball but the crowd made so much noise he couldn't hear us. Besides, he should have caught it without anybody yelling at him," asserted Muggsy.

The theme repeated itself in 1913. After helping the Giants to their third straight NL flag, Merkle belted New York's only homer of the World Series in the fourth game. In the fifth and final contest, Philadelphia cruised to the championship 3–1. All the runs scored on errors, including a miscue by Merkle. Once again, his rare mistake eclipsed all of his good plays.

Movin' On

In its 1916 pennant stretch drive, Brooklyn needed a replacement for its injured first baseman and traded for Merkle. He wound up playing sparingly but appeared in three World Series games. The Red Sox dominated the Robins four games to one.

Brooklyn sold Fred to the Cubs early in 1917 after Chicago first baseman Vic Saier broke his leg. Merkle, who had slipped a bit the last few years, righted his career and turned in three solid seasons as Chicago's regular first-sacker. He played well in the 1918 World Series, but young southpaw pitcher Babe Ruth and the Red Sox were too tough for the Cubs and won in six games.

All the years of bashing wore on Merkle. "Little slips that would be excused in other players are burned into me by the crowds," he confided in 1915.

Merkle tired of the majors and spent four hugely productive seasons with Rochester of the International League. He saved the best for last, slamming 22 homers and batting .351 in 1924.

The local press praised him for outworking his teammates, most of them 10 to 15 years younger. Merkle said he enjoyed those years, although—going by the articles written about him—he took more rather than less verbal abuse from the minor-league crowds. Heckling the infamous Bonehead Merkle was a way to show off one's baseball knowledge and get cheap yuks in the smaller towns.

Humble and modest by nature, Merkle was not a showman on the field. He made an exception in a game between Rochester and Jersey City in 1923. Jersey's catcher and hard-throwing pitcher—a pair of cocky loudmouths—kept yapping to Merkle that he couldn't hit the kid's fastball. The count was two balls and no strikes with runners on first and second.

The old pro calmly told the catcher that if the pitcher threw a fastball, he would not swing the bat but catch the ball with one bare hand and peg it right back to the pitcher. That's exactly what he did.

"It was an automatic strike, that's all. [The pitcher] swelled up and almost burst, he was so mad. He tried to hit me with the next pitch, but it went behind me," recalled Merkle, his humble-pie lesson not quite finished. "Then he delivered another pitch, and I tripled. He couldn't pitch after that."

The Yankees purchased Merkle from Rochester for $6,000 on June 17, 1925. They wooed him back to the bigs by paying him at the lavish rate of a $6,000 annual salary to serve as a coach and reserve player. Originally, Rochester requested a promising 21-year-old first baseman named Lou Gehrig as compensation. Well, it didn't hurt to ask. Fifteen days before Fred signed, Gehrig replaced slumping veteran Wally Pipp at first base. Merkle made only 18 plate appearances over the next year and a half. Gehrig the "Iron Horse" played every game for the next 14 years.

Fred did not appear in the 1926 Series but was on the roster. The Cardinals beat the Yankees in seven games, making the hard-luck Merkle 0-for-6 when his teams played in the World Series.

Management made coaching changes in the offseason and did not retain Merkle, leaving him one season shy of World Series glory as part of the "Murderers' Row" 1927 Yankees.

Glowing Record

For his career, Merkle hit .273 in 1,637 games and amassed 1,579 hits, 720 runs, 753 runs batted in, 271 stolen bases, eight seasons of 20 or more swipes and 14 steals of home. Only 20 players in the history of the game stole home more. A rare power-speed player who usually hit in the clean-up spot, he led four teams to pennants and contributed to two other league champs.

His stats are impressive in the context of the deadball era, but his contributions transcended his offensive numbers. Merkle's baseball smarts matched his high IQ. He was McGraw's sounding board almost from the start.

"McGraw never consulted anybody except Merkle on questions of strategy…. He never asked Matty, he never asked me. He'd say, 'Fred, what do you think of this?'" stated Meyers, a Giant for seven years beginning in 1909. Bonehead? "What a misnomer. One of the smartest men in baseball, Fred Merkle. Isn't that something? It just shows you what the newspapers can do to you."

As player-manager, Merkle tried to settle an unstable Reading team of the International League in 1927 but was let go in July, shortly after he lost his father to cancer.

In 1929, Fred gave managing another shot in his new hometown of Daytona Beach. A young hot-dog player made a bonehead crack. Enough. Quitting on the spot, Merkle simply turned and walked off the diamond.

The media and the public relentlessly ridiculed Merkle, but baseball people knew better. He was universally admired and respected by his big-league teammates as well as opposing players.

"I guess there's no doubt it's still the most famous play in the history of baseball. For Fred's sake, I wish it had never happened, it caused him so much grief," said Bridwell in his later years. "I wish I'd never gotten that hit that set off the whole Merkle incident. I wish I'd struck out instead. If I'd have done that, it would have spared Fred a lot of unfair humiliation."

Klem insisted that Evers "talked a great and good umpire (O'Day) into making the rottenest decision in the history of baseball. The intent in this rule applied to infield grounders and such. It does not apply to cleanly hit drives to the outfield that make a force-out impossible unless the runner on first drops dead."

Rotten indeed, but Klem's defense of the status quo was misguided. Then and ever since, outfielders successfully executed force-outs. The definition of an obvious hit with no chance of a force would be open to the interpretation of each umpire, leaving the same gray area as before. Right after the Gill play, baseball should have told its umpires to invoke Rule 59 in all such situations. Of course, it should have informed Merkle and everyone else first.

Instead, ignorance and confusion prevailed, and Merkle paid the price.

He rarely talked about the play or his plight, but he was painfully candid when he did.

"For years while I continued to play, it haunted me and kept me in constant fear of 'what can happen to me now,'" he admitted in 1950. "The fact of the matter is what I did was common practice in those days. The same thing probably had been done a half-dozen times during the season but nobody ever was called on it. The umpires decided to be technical just when I did it."

MERKLE FAMILY PHOTO. STANDING: ETHEL MERKLE, ERNST JOHN KARL MERKLE, EARNEST MERKLE, PASTOR WILLIAM BRENNER. SITTING: FRED MERKLE, ANNA MARIA THIELMANN, ANNA AMALIA MERKLE. CHILDREN: MARGIE MERKLE AND JEANNETTE MERKLE (MARIANNE NOT YET BORN).

After Baseball:
"The Measure of a Man..."

The measure of a man is the way he bears up under misfortune. —Plutarch

MERKLE CHAMPION RED BARBER

There was a lot more to Fred Merkle than the grim-faced player the fans saw on the field. Although Merkle resented the bonehead tag, he liked the life of a ballplayer. He enjoyed playing the game, rooming with the convivial Doyle and playing cards and chess with Matty and the gang.

Fred experienced the trip of a lifetime in the off-season of 1913-14. It was worthy of its billing as the "Tour to End All Tours." The Giants, the White Sox, several other top-notch players and an Olympian-turned ballplayer named Jim Thorpe played exhibition games in 13 countries—including Japan, China, the Philippines, Australia, Ceylon, Egypt, France and England—from October to March.

Amalia urged her son to marry Ethel and make the trip a honeymoon, just as Doyle did. Fred went by himself. Under increasing pressure from their mothers, the couple of eight years finally tied the knot a few months later.

"Both had a lot of baggage. My Dad obviously had the baseball stigma. Mom's natural father was an alcoholic who hanged himself when she was 12. Her mother quickly remarried for survival. The stepfather, a real creep, kicked the kids out of the house when my mother was 16. She went to work for a widower who had a daughter her age and lived in that home. Education was important to my mother, but she had to leave school in the 10th grade," explained youngest daughter Marianne.

In 1908—prior to the Merkle game—Ethel traveled to Bellingham, Washington, to visit the family of her half-sister. Everyone was excited to meet the girlfriend of a real big-league baseball player. Ethel made a return visit in 1910. All anyone wanted to know was whether she had dumped the guy with the bonehead nickname yet.

Fully accepting each other's baggage, Fred and Ethel committed themselves to being devoted spouses and parents for the next 42 years. Ethel gave birth to Jeannette in 1915 and Margie in 1917.

During the winters, Fred began carving out a life in Florida for himself and his family. He bought a house on the west side of the Halifax River in the small town of Ormond near Daytona Beach. John D. Rockefeller lived on the beach side next to a golf course, where Merkle and Rockefeller occasionally played together.

Merkle purchased a fruit farm in the same area. He enjoyed tending to the crops. Meanwhile, Ernst—now retired—and Amalia decided to move near their son and bought a house in Ormond.

Unlike many players, Fred had planned responsibly for his and his family's future. Life after baseball was looking mighty good.

Family's Trials and Triumphs

Then his whole world started to unravel all over again. In 1925, his parents' house burned to the ground. All of Fred's baseball possessions were stored there in a huge trunk and went up in smoke. Fortunately, Ernst and Amalia were not home when the blaze struck.

The stock-market crash in October 1929 brought on the Great Depression. Fred was forced to sell his farm at a substantial loss. Concurrently, his savings plunged.

In 1930, Merkle picked up the phone and called the many people in baseball who had promised him a job after his retirement. He was more than qualified for a coaching, scouting or front-office position. He hardly even got his calls returned. The Depression took its toll on baseball, too.

Fred took a menial job working on a Works Progress Administration, county bridge project. He could barely make ends meet on WPA wages, but with a family to support and millions of Americans out of work, some job was better than no job.

The Merkles then learned they were about to get a surprise visit from the stork 14 years after their last child. Their doctor, understanding the situation, discussed the option of putting the child up for adoption. No way. In 1931, Ethel gave birth to a third daughter, Marianne. Terrible timing aside, she would prove to be a godsend to both her parents and a kindred spirit to her father.

In the same year, the Merkles lost their house, which was a devastating blow to homemaker Ethel. A so-called friend of Fred's reneged on a verbal mortgage agreement and demanded the entire balance. Fred didn't even have the money to pay the real estate taxes.

The family would move three times in the next three years. In 1934, friends of Ethel's let the Merkles rent a 14-room house in a hot, buggy, remote area a mile further inland along the Halifax River, which was originally known as the North Mosquito River for good reason.

It was like living in a jungle. The property was nearly surrounded by tall grasses, vines, cacti and palmettos. Spiders, snakes and assorted critters were everywhere. The mosquitoes were so thick that Ethel wore a winter coat and scarf during the day when she had to get to the clothes-lines. Amalia, who lived there for four years, wrapped her legs in newspapers before taking her evening strolls.

The Merkles had to stay there for 14 years. These were difficult times for Ethel, who suffered two nervous breakdowns and ongoing panic attacks and stopped driv-ing after getting into several car accidents. She battled severe migraine headaches and needed the house to be almost pin-drop quiet. The girls all developed their own problems with migraines.

The agreement with the property owner called for Ethel to have the house ready to show to potential buy-ers at all times. Whenever she saw well-dressed people nearby, she assumed they were real estate agents. She ducked down and hid behind furniture and told her daughters to do likewise. Although the place was hardly ideal, Ethel would do all in her power to keep her family under that roof.

Fred's wife also was threatened by another breed of strangers. Tramps roamed the country during the Depres-sion. Ethel was terrified when they came near but always gave them something to eat, even if only a piece of bread. It was not uncommon for the Merkles to look out their windows at night and see a scraggly-looking group hud-dled around a fire. The term homeless people hadn't been coined yet.

"My mother knew what she was getting into, baseball-wise, when she married my father. But not about all the other stuff. She really didn't complain about anything but adjusted to situations as they arose. Arise, they did. She had a tough childhood and had learned to do without. That skill was put to use during the Depression years," said Marianne.

Baseball was a delicate topic. Kids in school made fun of the girls for having a bonehead father. Fred loved to tell old baseball stories, but they were never about himself or "the play." Reporters and family members alike knew better than to ask. Fred didn't even know his career batting average, and he rarely followed major-league baseball after his playing days. Any baseball mementos that Fred collected after the fire were not on display in the Merkle home.

STICKING TOGETHER

The family made the best of hard times by enjoying life's simple pleasures and each other. On the radio, they listened to quiz shows, dramas and, especially, music. Fred's favorite was the Budapest String Quartet. The parents and the girls loved to hear the Metropolitan Opera on Saturdays. Fred jokingly referred to Italian opera composer Giuseppe Verdi as "Joe Green." Ethel bought books about opera stories for Marianne. Fred explained the instruments and often translated German operas for her. Marianne learned all about the major conductors and operatic stars.

Every Merkle devoured books and magazines. The girls asked their parents questions, which led to fun, lively, informative discussions. Fred completed the Sunday newspaper's crossword puzzle no matter how long it took. He enjoyed Rudyard Kipling poems, Tarzan stories and the tales of Captain Horatio Hornblower in the *Saturday Evening Post*. He introduced Marianne to Sherlock Holmes mysteries, the short stories of O. Henry and sportswriters such as Ring Lardner. When the librarian would not let Marianne take out advanced books for adults, her father would have a talk with the lady and straighten her out.

Marianne suffered from whooping cough, asthma and rheumatic fever as a child and nearly died from bronchial pneumonia when she was in fifth grade. She frequently could not attend school for weeks, but her education was more rigorous at home. Ethel read nearly every one of Shakespeare's plays to her. When Marianne was in fourth grade, she read at a senior high level.

She also discovered how it felt to get "Merkled." Jeannette helped her little sister, home ill again, to prepare for a history contest. The teacher already had decided that another student—the daughter of the PTA president—was the winner, but Marianne's score tied her for first place. The solution? The school cancelled the contest.

Amalia taught Ethel how to cook Fred's favorite dishes. His very favorite was creamed codfish—which required overnight soakings and several rinsings—on baked potatoes. Amalia made mincemeat pies—Marianne's favorite. Fred did the grocery shopping. His special treat was to put vanilla ice cream in his coffee, a habit Marianne acquired and enjoyed with him. Fred's only turn at cooking was the occasional breakfast of fried eggs, bacon and coffee—which triggered a family ritual. He made boiled coffee and tossed in eggshells to settle the grounds, which always left a mess that brought howls from Ethel followed by giggles from the girls in the background.

Christmases were warm occasions with few material adornments. On Christmas Eve, Fred cut down a cedar tree and helped Ethel, Jeannette and Margie decorate it. When dusk turned dark, little Marianne was summoned to the living room to see the lit tree for the first time. Then it was silly time as all hands got busy forming animal shadows on the wall. Fred made popcorn by holding a little metal box over the fire in the fireplace. Everyone enjoyed Grandma Amalia's German Springerli cookies with raised designs. The limit per person was two gifts—usually a homemade doll and a book for Marianne. Jeannette, an artistic perfectionist, taught her little sister how to wrap gifts and make bows. Every scrap of paper was saved and carefully pressed for next year.

Fred wanted a better life for his family. It would not be easy. In 1936, he still had a lousy job and little money. He also got another rude reminder of his public image.

MERKLE WITH REDESIGNED FISHING FLOATS IN HIS SHOP

Merkle agreed to umpire an exhibition game between the Washington Senators and a minor-league team. A young wiseacre player called him that name that rhymes with conehead.

LIGHT, TUNNEL

Just as he did in his baseball career, Merkle kept on truckin'. He started a business manufacturing fishing floats from his home. His partner provided funding. A breakthrough came when Fred redesigned the float's insert tube from wood to brass in order to reduce soaking. The piece changed to plastic during World War II when metals for nonmilitary products became scarce.

The partners opened a small shop. As hoped, Fred's baseball name finally proved to be a blessing instead of a curse. Several competitors got out of the fishing business during the war, switching to military products. Merkle and his partner worked well together, and their market share steadily increased. Fred handled the bookkeeping and finances while his partner oversaw production. Eventually, they invested in a factory to meet the growing demand.

When she was 10 years old, Marianne could tell her father's business was picking up. "We went on a planned trip to the Orange Bowl. Dad bought me a clarinet, a small sailboat and a bike. He couldn't afford those things before," she recalled.

The father and his youngest daughter formed a special rapport. They both worked together as airplane spotters during the war years, sharing the graveyard shift from 2 a.m. to 6 a.m. several times. The room had to be totally quiet as they listened for planes. Fred occasionally broke the silence by singing "On the Road to Mandalay" and other tunes.

"He always said 'much obliged' to everyone instead of 'thank you.' He often greeted me with, 'Good Morning, Glory', which always made me smile," Marianne remembered.

Slowly but surely, life got better for the Merkles. The older daughters grew up and moved away. Jeannette recovered from tuberculosis and an 18-month stay in a sanatorium before settling in Los Angeles. Margie got married and had two sons. Under less stress, Ethel's emotions leveled out, and her headaches receded.

Fred found himself with more spare time and money in his pockets. In 1948, he moved the family to a comfortable second-story apartment in Daytona Beach. He played cards with his friends at a dinky little shack near the river in Ormond. They affectionately called it the "Yacht Club."

On Saturdays, he played bridge at the Elks Club in Daytona. Merkle occasionally brought his youngest daughter. "I considered it a very special time. We were served by the steward. A burger and the national salad of the time—iceberg lettuce, slices of tomato topped with the traditional dollop of mayo," Marianne reflected fondly.

She was acutely aware that someone might bring up you-know-what anytime, anyplace.

Marianne and her father attended their regular Lutheran church one Sunday. Two ministers visited from Toledo, one delivering part of the sermon. There was a brief shake-and-greet after the service. With his daughter at his side, Fred mentioned to the guest speaker that he also was from Toledo.

"Bonehead Merkle was from Toledo, too, but we don't claim him," cracked the pastor.

LURE OF THE GAME

Despite such brutal reminders, Merkle gravitated back to his favorite game in the late 1940s. When he read that Grover Hartley got the job to manage the Florida State League's Daytona Beach Islanders, he volunteered to help his old Giants' teammate. After quietly coaching the young players on fundamentals in several preseason practices, he attended every home game, blending into the crowd in his customary spot on a stool down the right-field line.

When the Brooklyn Dodgers clinched the 1949 National League flag, general manager Branch Rickey invited every living member of the franchise's 1916 pennant-winning team to the World Series games at Ebbets Field. Merkle looked up to Rickey, who arguably possessed the most astute baseball mind ever. Fred said he was tempted to accept but didn't feel well enough to make the trip. He was the only one who didn't show up.

Hall of Fame announcer Red Barber, noticing Fred's absence, saw an opportunity to right a long-time wrong. He knew that Merkle was about to receive an invitation from New York Giants' owner Horace Stoneham to attend an old-timers' game at the Polo Grounds the following summer.

Barber, also a columnist for the *New York Journal American,* wrote a series of impassioned articles about the injustice done to a good man, insisting it was high time for everyone to band together and do something about it. He visited Merkle in Florida and encouraged him to return to New York. Fred was noncommittal. Barber went on to Miami and interviewed Klem, who provided plenty of material by resuming his passionate defense of Merkle.

The invitation arrived. The old-timers of the Giants and Cardinals would play a three-inning exhibition game Sunday, July 30, 1950, before the current teams' regularly scheduled contest. Merkle would need to arrive Thursday night and attend a series of interviews and dinners through the weekend.

Ethel, burying the resentment she had felt toward baseball for more than four decades, encouraged her husband to return to the scene of the crime. Face the demons and purge them, once and for all.

Fred's daughter delivered the coup de grace. Marianne, now a pretty 19-year-old, told her father she had a vacation coming from her job as a switchboard operator and that she would love to go with him to New York. She knew how apprehensive Dad was. This would be a case of role reversal, the child providing moral support to the parent at every turn.

BETTER LATE THAN NEVER

New York's media followed Barber's lead.

"It's high time the fans and press of the present era atoned for the sins of a generation that used the incident

FRED MERKLE, DAUGHTER MARIANNE AND TEAMMATE LARRY DOYLE IN
NEW YORK FOR OLD TIMERS' WEEKEND IN 1950

to hound Merkle... It's up to the fans to make Fred feel, not that he has been forgiven but that there is nothing to forgive unless it is the sins of their predecessors, who were so cruel to him."

—Dan Parker, *Daily Mirror*, July 28, 1950.

Merkle was eating breakfast with his daughter in the hotel dining room that Friday. A familiar-looking man with gray hair was seated nearby. "If you think you know him, why don't you go over and introduce yourself," urged Marianne.

"So it's you, Fred!" shouted Laughin' Larry Doyle, shrugging off his long battle with tuberculosis. The long-time roommates hadn't seen each other in 25 years. They hugged and were virtually inseparable the rest of the weekend, culminated by a Sunday night reunion dinner at Toots Shor's.

The biggest interview was the first. Merkle appeared Friday on a national radio program—NBC's "We the People." He was greeted by Blanche McGraw. John's widow took the microphone and proceeded to hit a grand-slam home run.

"To me, this is a great injustice to a great ball player and a fine gentleman. Fred, we miss you in New York. You were one of John's best boys. They couldn't write the history of baseball without reserving a big, glowing chapter for a brilliant first baseman named Fred Merkle. And from here on, all of us will remember the big boner involving Fred Merkle was the public's boner—the boner of forgetting to honor its great star."

Barber wrote about how touched he was to receive two unexpected visitors over the weekend. "I mailed the columns to Merkle and went my way with the Dodgers. Ballplayers don't write. Merkle didn't. Then, too, maybe he didn't appreciate my stirring it all up again. I was at Brooklyn, which was another world from Manhattan...when Merkle and one of his daughters walked (into his office). His daughter said, 'We wanted to come by and thank you. If you hadn't written those columns, we wouldn't be here.' "

All of the former Giants were in uniform Sunday, except for the two oldest—Merkle and Doyle, each wearing suits. One by one, legends such as Carl Hubbell and Mel Ott emerged from the dugout and took bows. The last man introduced was Merkle. The crowd of 35,073 gave him the loudest and longest ovation.

The follow-up stories served as exclamation points. "I boil every time I hear some silly jerk talk about (Merkle's) bonehead play. The one talking about it is the bonehead, not Merkle. Every intelligent person who was around back in 1908 knows it was the custom not to bother touching second base on such a play. Merkle was just unlucky enough to be the fall guy the first time the rule was enforced," said Lester Bromberg, *The Sporting News,* August 9, 1950.

Was it enough? Of course not. Forty-two years of public flogging didn't disappear because of one feel-good weekend. But it sure helped.

GOLDEN YEARS

Fred got more involved in baseball back in Florida. In 1954, he umpired games in the State Negro Baseball Tournament. Merkle was impressed with an 18-year-old pitcher and wanted to tout him to his friend Hank Greenberg, the Hall of Fame slugger who was now general manager of the Cleveland Indians. Jim "Mudcat" Grant was even more impressed with Merkle.

"He said, 'I don't know if I should recommend you or not. My name could work against you,' " recalled Grant. The young hurler would receive Merkle's endorsement, sign with Greenberg's Indians for $100, win 145 big-league games and pitch in the World Series and two All-Star games. After his career, Grant dedicated himself to promoting the history of blacks in baseball. He's never forgotten Merkle.

"He was anything but a bonehead. He was one of the nicest men I ever met. He was always at my side, ready to help me. He was supposed to get a bonus if the Indians called me up. (They gave it to Ethel after Fred passed away.) Merkle deserved to get something out of baseball. He sure gave it a lot."

Bernard Kahn, a close friend and the sports editor of the *Daytona Beach News-Journal,* asked Fred to help out when the newspaper began to sponsor youth baseball clinics in 1950. Merkle adored kids and enjoyed coaching them, but—even after the weekend in New York—he was still wary about being on a baseball diamond in the public eye. Ultimately, he accepted the invitation.

"He was a superb instructor and when the clinic ended, all Fred said to me was 'thanks.' As he turned to go to his car, there were tears in his eyes," remembered Kahn after the first session.

The *Baltimore Sun's* Lou Hatter asked Merkle how he could befriend any sportswriter after the whole lot of them hung him in effigy as a 19-year-old. "I hold no resentment toward newspapermen, either, as a class. Some of my best friends are sportswriters," stated Merkle.

Fred was able to retire from the fishing business in 1953, three years before his death. Because of his perseverance, Merkle made his life progressively better during the 1940s, and it was actually pretty darned sweet his last six years.

Merkle died in his sleep of natural causes on March 2, 1956, at age 67. Protecting his privacy, the family buried him in an unmarked grave.

The major newspapers predictably reverted to form in their obituaries and tied Merkle's legacy to one play 48 years prior. In the *New York Times:* "Giant First Baseman's 'Boner' in Failing to Touch 2nd Led to Loss of '08 Pennant."

Fred knew that's how it would go and even joked about it: "I suppose when I die, they'll put on my tombstone, 'Here Lies Bonehead Merkle.'"

"Merkle wasn't bitter when he died, because by nature, he was a kindly person who loved kids and, deep down, loved baseball," said Kahn. "I knew Fred well. He was a wonderful person. He and his family paid a terrible price for that 1908 play. He took the almost uncalled rap in sports, without ever defending himself."

MERKLE'S LEGACY:
HERO, EMPOWERING
ROLE MODEL

BROOKLYN ROBINS' FRED MERKLE—SAFE AT HOME!

Marianne, now 79, is a lot like her Dad. She has battled through considerable adversity in her own life, starting with her difficult childhood. Everyone in the Merkle family has had to grapple with the bonehead stigma, but it was Marianne who fought the beast head-on at a young age on behalf of her father.

After Fred passed away, Marianne decided to put herself through school. All on her own, she became the first college graduate of the three daughters. Although that would have made her father proud, it was never a priority of his. Young women were supposed to get married and raise a family.

Marianne did that, too. She married John Kasbaum. They have daughter Kathy (Hubbard), 45, and son Phillip, 34, but lost another daughter, Jennifer, to meningitis when she was just three years old. Marianne's migraine headaches finally went away when she turned 50. John has been ill in recent years. The cost of his medical care took big bites out of their family savings and monthly living budget. The Kasbaums downsized and moved into a small apartment in the Los Angeles area. Marianne never complains. She wears life's scars and looks forward to the next day. Just like Dad.

Comcast SportsNet released an award-winning video documentary of the "Fred Merkle Story" on September 23, 2008—the centennial date of the famous game. It's divided into two parts and available on YouTube. Coincidentally, the Cubs visited the National League's New York team—the Mets—that day. Just as eerily, Brant Brown dropped a fairly routine fly ball on September 23, 1998, that cost the Cubs a loss to the Brewers and elicited anguished "Oh, no" cries from Chicago radio announcer and former Cubs' star Ron Santo. The Cubbies wound up qualifying for the postseason by winning a one-game playoff—over the Giants, naturally.

Marianne granted a rare phone interview for the Comcast feature. The pain in her voice was evident, but her words were not bitter or blameful. She confided, "You just never knew who was going to say what when. Other people have celebrities in their families, and they can use it...and sort of enjoy it. We could never do that. So it was just always there."

Sue Baxter, Merkle's grandniece, found out about "it" the hard way when she was a little girl. Only vaguely aware of her famous relative and the play, she asked about "the play" in the middle of a family gathering "It was like somebody died," she recalled.

The impact of that experience kicked in two decades later. Baxter saw a reprint of a 1909 Fred Merkle card in a card shop and knew she had to have it. That led to more cards, more memorabilia and intense research. She soon found herself copying articles at the National Baseball Hall of Fame's library in Cooperstown. Her vast Merkle memorabilia collection was on display at her hometown library in Findlay, Ohio, a few years ago. It keeps growing.

"Along the way, I learned that what he did wasn't unusual and that he got a bum deal. I am very proud of my grand uncle. This became a hobby that I enjoy very much, but it's also a passion. I took it upon myself to clear his name," explained Baxter, who refuses to use the bonehead word "out of respect for him."

Merkle's is a comfortable, well-run sports bar that opened in Chicago's flourishing Wrigleyville neighborhood in 2004. When Sue heard about it, she was understandably skeptical of the proprietors' motives in naming the bar. A friend went on a reconnaissance mission and visited the establishment. The menu devoted a full page to Fred's story. The friend spoke to one of the two partners. The young entrepreneur seemed to understand that Merkle was a victim. The owners simply picked the catchy name of a player linked to the Cubs and baseball history. For the most part, the young clientele didn't know or care who Merkle was.

Conversely, David Stalker really, really cares. Outside of Fred's family, Dave is the world's No. 1 Merkle fan. Stalker and his wife Lynne live in Watertown, Wisconsin—Fred's birthplace. It's a special treat for fans of baseball history when Dave exhibits his extensive collection of deadball era memorabilia, nearly half of which is devoted solely to Merkle.

Joining with the Merkle family in raising money, David spearheaded a campaign to erect a memorial monument on the land of Watertown's historical society. The dedication took place in 2005. Watertown's park district then got in the spirit and re-named a local diamond Fred Merkle Field.

There is deliberately no mention of September 23, 1908, on the black-marble structure. The words focus on Merkle's background and career accomplishments.

"Fred Merkle was anything but a bonehead. He played the game that day the way everyone had played it up to that point. The casual person who walks by the monument goes, 'Wow, here's a guy from Watertown who was on six World Series teams.' That's what he should be remembered for," said Stalker, who has since honored 10 more deadball-era players from the Midwest with memorials and intends to expand the nonprofit effort into a national series.

Many members of the highly regarded Society for American Baseball Research have written accounts of the Merkle affair and exonerated him of any wrongdoing. SABR's foremost Merkle contributor has been political commentator and former sports anchor Keith Olbermann. The man with the prickly reputation who makes many see red turns into a puddle of sympathy on the subject of Merkle. For years, he wrote articles about Merkle every September 23rd. He has proposed September 23 as a national day of amnesty in Fred's honor.

"The rules sometimes change while you're playing the game. Those you trust to tell you the changes often don't bother to. The (Merkle) saga has always seemed to me to be a microcosm not just of baseball, nor of celebrity but of life," wrote Olbermann in the foreword to Anderson's *More than Merkle.*

He continued, "That for which history still mocks you would have gone unnoticed if you had done it a month or a day before."

MERKLE'S PLIGHT: PRIMARY CAUSES

Authority betrayal, circumstance and scapegoating are the main factors that conspired against Fred. Olbermann identified the first two.

A system has a set of rules. Someone in power changes them and doesn't let the participants know beforehand. That's authority betrayal.

Merkle veered toward the clubhouse because that was baseball custom on an obvious game-ending hit to the outfield. If anyone had told him that umpires were going to start calling the play in accordance with Rule 59, he would have continued and touched second base.

We've all been there in some way. A parent, a teacher, a coach or a boss changed a rule and didn't inform us first. We behaved according to the old rule and had no knowledge that there was a new rule. We were punished for it.

The difference is obvious. Comparatively speaking, our unjust penance was minor. Merkle performed on the grand stage and paid the ultimate price of extreme public ignominy.

Fred also was victimized by circumstance or fate. Circumstance involves conditions affecting a person by sheer chance or luck. Fate is a scarier concept to ponder because it entails an external power or a force of destiny controlling the events. Whichever it was, numerous events had to take place before, during and after September 23, 1908—and in the exact order in which they occurred—to place Merkle on the chopping block.

First of all, it's surprising Fred chose to play baseball out of high school instead of attending college. He was highly intelligent and intellectually curious. He could have been a doctor, lawyer, writer, teacher or engineer.

He chose baseball and excelled at it, but he had played only on the Class D level, and getting discovered by talent scouts was a very iffy proposition back then. Brush just happened to be in Michigan and just happened to go to a barber who knew about Merkle. That placed him with the big-market New York Giants and the largest, most aggressive core of sportswriters.

He made the team instead of being sent to the high minors for more seasoning. He nearly died and lost a foot to amputation that summer. The NL pennant race had to go precisely the way it did before, on and after September 23rd. The sportswriters, Pulliam, O'Day, Emslie, McGraw, Mathewson, Tenney, Evers, Bridwell and others had to play their roles exactly as they did in every situation.

The biggest irony of all was Fred's wise baseball decision not to stretch his single into a double. He said he could have made it easily, but—with the winning run on third—it wasn't worth the risk. If Merkle had been on second base, he would not have been subject to a force-out, and the whole furor never would have occurred at all. His smart play before the fateful play put him in harm's way.

Change any one of these events, or the order in which they occurred, and Merkle escapes infamy.

GET YOUR GOAT

Scapegoating is the practice of laying blame for an undesirable outcome on one person and one play while

ignoring all the other factors contributing to that outcome. Playing the blame game always has been the
easy, convenient thing for sportswriters to do, and fans
tend to hop right on board.

The size of the goat horns depends on several conditions. John Billheimer, who wrote *Baseball and the Blame
Game: Scapegoating in the Major Leagues,* looked at numerous
players who have been branded over the years. He determined the five primary elements that condemn a player to
the harshest treatment. The player who is a superstar gets
off more lightly. A mental error or perceived mental error
draws more wrath than a physical mistake. Coverage of
the game by the East Coast press tends to be more severe.
Did the play in question occur in the late innings? Did the
player's team lose a lead?

Bingo. Poor Fred was the only one of all the scapegoats to score a "perfect" 5-for-5.

Additionally, Merkle's timing made him uniquely
vulnerable. In the early fall of 1908, baseball took center stage, but it was still relatively new, its leaders neither
savvy nor well-organized. The Gill play was one of those
rulebook-versus-tradition situations that begged for reso-
lution but instead found the heads of the sport's officials
buried in sand.

Editors let muckraker-style sportswriters write virtually anything they wanted, their zeal to sell newspapers
completely outweighing any sense of fairness toward one
young player.

Overwhelmed by a confluence of world-changing events, the typical American of the era was excited, confused—and, frankly—somewhat schizophrenic. Our people presented themselves as morally upright, but that didn't quite square with their history of treating minorities, immigrants, women and even their own children badly. The average fan gravitated to baseball but wasn't yet very knowledgeable about the game, tending to trust in the sport's leaders and believe whatever the newspapers said.

Fred's veer-off was accepted, ingrained baseball custom, but most people didn't realize that, and the rest didn't care. The result was that everyone from baseball officials to the press to the fans behaved ignorantly. Everyone acted like a bonehead except Merkle, which is another of his story's striking ironies.

Some observers feel that nothing close to the trashing of Merkle can ever happen again because we live in more sophisticated, enlightened times. No, the practice of scapegoating lives on.

Boston's Bill Buckner let a bouncer go through his legs in the sixth game of the 1986 World Series. The Mets won that game and the next one to win the Series. The creaky-kneed Buckner, who was toward the end of an outstanding career, shouldn't have even been on the field at the time. After years of tolerating humiliation and exile, Buckner was brought back by the Red Sox and forgiven by their fans only after the team won the 2004 Series to end its 86-year drought.

Cubs' fan Steve Bartman reached out for and touched a foul fly that left-fielder Moises Alou could have caught. He had played some ball as a youngster and coached a good youth travel all-star team in Chicago's northwest suburbs. He did what the average fan does reflexively, but he also should have known better. The batter reached base, and the Cubs completely imploded. The Florida Marlins made a huge comeback to win the sixth game of the 2003 National League Championship Series. They won the next game and then the World Series. Bartman was harassed out of the park by the fans, Fox TV's on-the-scene Dane Placko describing a lynch-mob mentality. The media immediately "outed" his identity and hounded him at his home and workplace. He was an international Internet joke within 12 hours. In an understatement, his punishment far exceeded his "crime." He has stayed away from the public eye ever since.

The difference is that Merkle had it a whole lot worse than Buckner or Bartman. Buckner retreated to Idaho and then got off the hook after less than two decades. Fred's cloud hung over him for the rest of his life. Bartman, a fan instead of a player, never had to ask himself whether he could perform on the field again and deal with the taunts and stares. Merkle mustered the strength to play on baseball's biggest stages for another 18 years.

JUST DUE: HERO, ROLE MODEL

Thanks to the efforts of Red Barber, David Stalker, Sue Baxter and many others, it appears Merkle finally has been vindicated. All of the contemporary experts have found him "innocent," which is quite a turnabout from the consensus of their counterparts more than a century ago.

"They inferred that he was stupid when, as we know, this is what most any player would have done," said Tim Wiles, director of research for baseball's Hall of Fame, in the Comcast piece.

"The one thing everyone seems to agree on is that Merkle was virtually blameless," Billheimer noted.

Christopher Bell, who wrote *Scapegoats: Baseballers Whose Careers Are Marked by One Fateful Play,* is among those who called Merkle a hero for what he endured.

Fred certainly qualifies as a hero. Unlike nearly every one of baseball's other foremost scapegoats, he did no wrong, yet he was the one who was stomped on the hardest. He fully understood that dichotomy and how unjustly he was treated, yet he carried on through unimaginable adversity.

The best kind of hero is also a role model. Merkle wasn't quite an elite player, but he was a superstar as a human being.

From the world of sports, there's never been a better role model in terms of fending off and rising above adversity. Outside of those players who died or suffered serious physical disabilities, Merkle is the unluckiest player in the history of baseball. No one ever got a rawer deal.

He didn't fold. He carried on and made the best of it. He didn't go around sulking or blaming others. He remained an exemplary teammate in every way. Merkle was a model of fortitude, perseverance, class and dignity.

Was he perfect? No. It took nearly a year for Fred to snap out of his funk after the initial public branding. He quit that last managing job in Daytona on the spot after hearing one too many bonehead cracks. But, all things considered, Merkle proved magnificent in confronting and surmounting more hardships than any player until Jackie Robinson came along.

Fred had to muster more resolve after his baseball career. The Great Depression bashed him hard. The betrayal by another cost him his house. Climbing out of a deep hole, he built a successful business and fought through severe adversity again.

He is not the only inspirational role model in this story. Marianne and the rest of Merkle's family all felt the brunt of Fred's unfair public humiliation and heard bonehead insults from others. They banded together to get through extremely hard times. The current generation of Merkles carries on the family's rock-solid values—rising above life's challenges and injustices and looking past the ignorance and cruelty of others.

Merkle understood that life is precious, short and unpredictable. Some of us are luckier than others. Fred was dealt a horribly bad hand but managed to make the very best of his life. He shook off depression, self-pity and bitterness. He did not allow the perceptions of others to define who he was. He kept his mind, soul and inner spirit bright and alive so that he could still be productive, enrich others and enjoy his own life.

His story is certainly not one of sorrow, regrets or failure. He always will represent a triumph of the human spirit. A great man emerged from 1908 and the crazy, wonderful madness of America, baseball, the dramatic pennant races and two of the sport's most memorable games. He was just a rookie when life blindsided him. He got back up, stood tall and passed the sternest test imaginable in a battle with adversity. Fred Merkle was a member of the 1908 New York Giants, but he left a permanent imprint and took one for a much bigger team.

A century later, as we all deal with our own setbacks and problems in life, Fred's example—"Merkle Power"— lives on.

FRED MERKLE MONUMENT—WATERTOWN, WISCONSIN

– EPILOGUE –

Excerpted from: "An Open Letter to Merkle's Grandson," Bernard Kahn, *Daytona Beach News-Journal,* March 5, 1956.

Rev. Paul Edris, pastor of the First Presbyterian Church in Daytona and a friend of Merkle's, wrote this to Freddie Robinson, Margie's son, three days after his grandfather passed away:

> *Dear Freddie: I don't know you...but I hear that you are 15 years old and like to play baseball. I also hear that a fellow made a crack at you not long ago about your granddaddy's "bonehead" and that it made you angry and hurt your mother's feelings.*
>
> *It hurts her feelings because she knows how heavy a burden your Granddaddy carried for over 40 years, because of one play that brought him that nickname. And she also knows it was undeserved.*
>
> *Now here is where I, a total stranger, want to put in my two cents' worth. You see, because I was Fred Merkle's friend. I know about the burden and I also know, as he knew and as everyone came to understand in these last few years, that it was totally undeserved. But I also know what it did to his family through the years and I don't want it ever to do it to you.*
>
> *So I want you to see this thing straight right now.*
>
> *Freddie, your granddaddy was a man. A real man.*

He carried the hurt of injustice inside him, for the most part, all those years. He never lashed back at the people who followed the crowd, which can often be cruel, and who hung the name 'bonehead' on him. He didn't let it throw him, either. After that famous play in 1908, he played big league baseball...for nearly 20 years.

He took the ribbing of the fans in stride. He wasn't one of the outstanding stars of the game. But he is remembered by those who played with him and those who managed him as a team player, a hard worker, and a very valuable man to have around when the going was tough and the pressure was on. He was a man with ice water in his veins. He never got rattled.

And he wasn't rattled, Freddie, on September 23, 1908, when the play happened. Bill Klem, Grantland Rice, Red Barber and many others have conclusively shown, in their writings and statements, that the play in which he got his nickname was a perfectly good play. It was the ruling on the play that was the "boner."

(McGraw) didn't talk him back to self-confidence and keep him on the Giants all those years, or become one of his closest friends, because he thought he was a bonehead. Who do you think was one of the first to visit your grandmother when news of your granddaddy's death was announced? Mrs. McGraw was with your grandmother when I got there.

Fred Merkle was a big, quiet man who loved to think, loved quiet pleasures and loved kids. He was the kind of man you and I can admire. He liked dependability and integrity and he liked his friends for themselves and not for what he might get out of them.

So here is my suggestion to you, Freddie....If there is ever any occasion for this 'bonehead' business to come up, just say, "Yes, sir, my granddaddy was Bonehead Merkle. Just call me Bonehead. I want to be the kind of bonehead he was."

– SOURCES –

Allen, Lee, *The National League Story,* New York: Hill & Wang, 1961.

Anderson, Dave, *Pennant Races,* New York: BBS Publishing, 1997.

Anderson, David W., *More than Merkle,* Lincoln; University of Nebraska, Press, 2000.

Bell, Christopher, *Scapegoats: Baseballers Whose Careers Are Marked by One Fateful Play,* Jefferson, NC: McFarland, 2002.

Billheimer, John, *Baseball and the Blame Game: Scapegoating in the Major Leagues,* Jefferson, NC: McFarland, 2007.

Burns, Ken, Baseball: A Film by Ken Burns, nine-part video documentary, produced originally for Public Broadcast Service, 1994.

Cooper, John Milton Jr., *Pivotal Decades: The United States, 1900-20,* New York: W. W. Norton, 1990.

Durso, Joseph, *Baseball and the American Dream,* St. Louis, Missouri: The Sporting News Publishing, 1986.

Evers, Jon and Hugh Fullerton, *Touching Second: The Science of Baseball,* Chicago, Reilly & Britton Company, 1912.

Fleming, G. H., *The Unforgettable Season,* New York: Penguin, 1981.

Garfien, Chuck, "Fred Merkle Story" video centennial documentary, Chicago: Comcast SportsNet, September 23, 2008.

Gilbert, Thomas, *Dead Ball: Major League Baseball Before Babe Ruth,* New York: Franklin Watts, 1996.

Honig, Donald, *Baseball America: The Heroes of the Game and the Times of Their Glory,* New York: Macmillan, 1985.

Hynd, Noel, *The Giants of the Polo Grounds,* New York: Doubleday, 1988.

James, Bill, *The New Bill James Historical Baseball Abstract,* New York: Free Press, 2001.

Jones, David, editor, *Deadball Stars of the American League,* Dulles, Virginia: Potomac Books, Society for American Baseball Research, 2006.

Kahn, Bernard, selected articles, *Daytona Beach News-Journal,* 1950-64.

Lieb, Frederick, *Baseball As I Have Known It,* New York: Coward, McCann & Geoghegan, 1977.

Mathewson, Christy, and John Wheeler, *Pitching in a Pinch,* Lincoln: University of Nebraska Press, 1994.

McCabe, Neil; McCabe, *Constance, Baseball's Golden Age: The Photographs of Charles M. Conlon,* St. Louis, Missouri: The Sporting News Publishing, 1993.

Murphy, Cait, *Crazy '08,* New York: HarperCollins, 2007.

Nemec, David; Wisnia, Saul, *Baseball: More Than 150 Years,* Lincolnwood, Illinois: Publications International, 1996.

Okrent, Daniel; Lewin, Harris; Nemec, David, *The Ultimate Baseball Book,* Boston: Houghton Mifflin, 2000.

Olbermann, Keith, lead article; fellow SABR contributors, special Merkle-centennial edition, Society for American

Baseball Research "The Inside Game" newsletter, September 23, 2008.

Rasenberger, Jim, *America 1908: The Dawn of Flight, the Race to the Pole, the Invention of the Model T and the Making of a Modern Nation,* New York: Scribner, 2007.

Reichler, Joseph, *The Baseball Encyclopedia: The Complete and Official Record of Major League Baseball,* New York: Macmillan, 1982.

Ritter, Lawrence, *The Glory of Their Times,* New York: Macmillan, 1966.

Seymour, Harold, *Baseball: The Golden Years,* New York: Oxford University Press, 1971.

Silverman, Al, editor, *The World of Sport: The Best from SPORT Magazine,* New York: Holt, Rinehart and Winston, 1948.

Simon, Tom, editor, *Deadball Stars of the National League,* Washington, D. C.: Brassey's, Society for American Baseball Research, 2004.

Stout, Glenn; Johnson, Richard, editor, *The Cubs: The Complete Story of Chicago Cubs Baseball,* Boston: Houghton Mifflin, 2007.

Thorn, John, *Baseball's 10 Greatest Games,* New York: Four Winds Press, 1981.

– Photograph Credits –

All photographs are reproduced with permission from the sources shown below.

Page	Photo Description	Source
i	Fred Merkle	National Baseball Hall of Fame Library Cooperstown, N.Y.
xiv	Early Merkle Trading Card	American Tobacco Company, Library of Congress
1	Wilbur Wright in Flight	George Grantham Bain Collection, Library of Congress
3	Ellis Island Scene	Library of Congress
5	Early Model T	Courtesy of Ford Motor Company
13	Theodore Roosevelt	Library of Congress
18	Harry Wright	National Baseball Hall of Fame Library Cooperstown, N.Y.
19	Vendor Sales Outside Ebbets Field	Library of Congress
30	John McGraw	George Grantham Bain Collection, Library of Congress
36	Larry Doyle	George Grantham Bain Collection, Library of Congress
37	Fred Merkle Throwing	National Baseball Hall of Fame Library Cooperstown, N.Y.
44	Cubs Infield Featuring Harry Steinfeldt, Joe Tinker, Johnny Evers and Frank Chance	National Baseball Hall of Fame Library Cooperstown, N.Y.

PAGE	PHOTO DESCRIPTION	SOURCE
45	Mordecai Brown	National Baseball Hall of Fame Library Cooperstown, N.Y.
52	Mike Donlin	George Grantham Bain Collection, Library of Congress
58	Honus Wagner	George Grantham Bain Collection, Library of Congress
62	National Baseball Commission	Library of Congress
63	Hank O'Day	George Grantham Bain Collection, Library of Congress
78	Johnny Evers	George Grantham Bain Collection, Library of Congress
79	Merkle	National Baseball Hall of Fame Library Cooperstown, N.Y.
88	Christy Mathewson	National Baseball Hall of Fame Library Cooperstown, N.Y.
89	Fred Merkle Batting	National Baseball Hall of Fame Library Cooperstown, N.Y.
101	Detroit Free Press Scoreboard Street Scene	George Grantham Bain Collection, Library of Congress
104	Ed Reulbach	George Grantham Bain Collection, Library of Congress
114	Polo Grounds Crowd Watching and Fans Leaving	George Grantham Bain Collection, Library of Congress
115	John Brush	George Grantham Bain Collection, Library of Congress
120	Bill Klem	Library of Congress

PAGE	PHOTO DESCRIPTION	SOURCE
129	Frank Chance	Paul Thompson Photographer, Library of Congress
136	Merkle, Wilson and Herzog	National Baseball Hall of Fame Library Cooperstown, N.Y.
137	Fred Merkle	National Baseball Hall of Fame Library Cooperstown, N.Y.
146	Merkle Family Photo	Merkle Family
147	Red Barber	Library of Congress
155	Merkle with Redesigned Floats in His Shop	Library of Congress
160	Merkle, Marianne and Doyle	Merkle Family
165	Fred Merkle Safe at Home	National Baseball Hall of Fame Library Cooperstown, N.Y.
178	Fred Merkle Monument in Watertown, Wisconsin	David Stalker

– INDEX –